COMMENTARY
—— on the ——
LETTER OF JAMES

Publishers

WATCHTOWER BIBLE AND TRACT SOCIETY
OF NEW YORK, INC.

INTERNATIONAL BIBLE STUDENTS ASSOCIATION
Brooklyn, New York, U.S.A.

First Edition
1,000,000 Copies

NOTE: Unless otherwise indicated, Bible quotations in this
book are from the modern-language *New World Translation of the Holy Scriptures*, revised edition of 1971.

Made in the United States of America

TABLE OF CONTENTS
James

Introduction
to The Letter of James

THE Letter of James is a call to practical Christianity on the part of all claiming to have faith in Christ. Evidence indicates that the James who penned this powerful Christian document was not an apostle, but was the half brother of the Lord Jesus Christ. (See comments on chapter 1.) James must have written his letter sometime prior to 62 C.E. In this year, according to the Jewish historian Josephus, High Priest Ananus, a Sadducee, was responsible for bringing James before the Sanhedrin and then having him stoned to death. Some scholars believe that the date of James' writing was about 60 C.E.*

The place of writing is generally agreed to have been Jerusalem. All the Scriptural testimony is to the effect that James was a resident of Jerusalem, remaining there, while the apostles engaged in carrying the message of Christianity to other parts of the earth. James is shown as being prominent in the Jerusalem congregation. (Acts 12:17; 15:13; 21:18; 1 Cor. 15:7; Gal. 1:19; 2:9, 12) His letter is referred to as a "general epistle" because it was not addressed to any specific congregation or person, as were most of the letters of the apostle Paul and Second and Third John.

According to the information provided in the wording of the letter, as well as other Biblical evidence, the Christian congregation was firmly established and Christian doctrine had been clearly set forth. Congregations had been formed all over the then civilized world, as shown in the book of Acts and in the letters of Paul and Peter.

---

* F. J. A. Hort, according to R. V. G. Tasker's *Commentary on the General Epistle of James*, p. 32.

Even James' salutation is a confirmation of this, being directed to "the twelve tribes [of spiritual Israel] that are *scattered about*."—Jas. 1:1.

James attacks several problems that had arisen in the congregations. One that caused much trouble was the misunderstanding and misconstruing by some persons of the doctrine of the free gift of righteousness through faith. (Rom. 5:15-17) These individuals mistakenly claimed that a Christian, having faith, did not need works—that faith had nothing to do with works. They overlooked the fact that true faith would show itself in some form of action. They were thereby denying that Christ "gave himself for us that he might deliver us from every sort of lawlessness and cleanse for himself a people peculiarly his own, zealous for *fine works*." (Titus 2:14) James was contending with the idea held by some Christians that a purely intellectual faith was sufficient for the Christian. This would ignore any need for faith to affect the heart, and would deny that faith had power to move a person to make changes in his personality and his life and to do things for others in positive expression of that faith. They were, if they maintained this idea, becoming like those of whom Paul speaks as having "a form of godly devotion but proving false to its power." —2 Tim. 3:5.

It should not be understood that James argued against the doctrine of righteousness "apart from works of law," which teaching the apostle Paul clearly defines in Romans chapters three and four. (Rom. 3:28) James' comments and counsel on Christian conduct always rest on the basis of "the faith of our Lord Jesus Christ." (Jas. 2:1) James was not in any way saying that works of themselves can bring salvation. We cannot properly devise a formula or build a structure through which we can work out our salvation. The faith must be there first. As James clearly emphasized, good works will come spontaneously from the heart, with the right motive of helping people in love and compassion. Jesus' life is an illustration of this. The law that the Christian follows is "the law of a free people," not a law code like the Mosaic law. (Jas. 2:12; Rom. 2:29; 7:6; 2 Cor. 3:6) It is the divine law that is written on the Christian's heart.—Jer. 31:33; Heb. 8:10.

As James shows, no Christian should judge his brother or set up human standards for gaining salvation, though he may encourage a brother and incite him to fine works; and he may even reprove his brother where there is definite Scriptural reason and Scriptural proof for what he says. (Jas. 4:11, 12; Gal. 6:1; Heb. 10:24) When the right works are performed they must be carried out in response to direction from God's Word. The real Christian will not do things by rote, and he does not need a detailed code of rules. Neither does he carry out his good works just to please men. So if a person has a genuine, living faith, fine works will reasonably follow, including preaching and teaching the good news of the Kingdom. (Matt. 24:14; 28:19, 20) They will be good works that God will reward, because they are performed out of heart devotion. However, one who tries to gain righteousness through a minutely defined structure of "dos" and "don'ts" will fail. Such "righteousness" is of men and not of God.

The Jews fell into this snare. "Because of not knowing the righteousness of God but seeking to establish their own, they did not subject themselves to the righteousness of God." (Rom. 10:3) The apostle Paul here means that the Jews tried to gain righteousness by works of law instead of grasping God's provided means of righteousness, Jesus Christ. (Rom. 3:21, 22) Their form of worship made the word of God of no effect. (Matt. 15:6, 9) Jesus said of the Jewish leaders: "They bind up heavy loads and put them upon the shoulders of men, but they themselves are not willing to budge them with their finger."—Matt. 23:4.

It is clear that James wrote to correct irregularities that had sprung up in the congregations at that time. Yet his letter applies with equal force in every age. In addition to his corrective counsel, James supports the writings of the apostles, and further clarifies the real nature of true worship as dynamic, affecting the heart and entire life and personality, as well as the intellect. By means of hard-hitting illustrations, he shows that religion without morality and without practical value in helping a person's fellowman is dead in God's eyes. One Bible commentator makes this significant point:

> "Whenever faith does not issue in love, and dogma, however orthodox, is unrelated to life; whenever Christians are tempted to settle down to a self-centered religion, and become oblivious to the social and material needs of others; or whenever they deny by their manner of living the creed they profess, and seem to be more anxious to be the friends of the world than friends of God, the Epistle of James has something to say to them which they disregard at their peril."*

But there is another fine aspect to James' letter that fills an ever-present need for Christians in every place, for it points out how a Christian can undergo trials and come out successful, victorious. There is great comfort in James' words for the person suffering from temptations, pressures and persecution. James wrote at a time when Christians not only were undergoing strong persecution, but were approaching a time when, as far as Christians were concerned, the affairs of the Roman nation would be more turbulent.

In only a short time after James wrote, Christians in Rome would be falsely blamed by Roman

---

* *The Tyndale New Testament Commentaries,* "The General Epistle of James," by R. V. G. Tasker, p. 10, par. 2.

Emperor Nero for the great fire of 64 C.E. that would destroy much of that city. Of course, this would lead to the persecution of Christians throughout the empire. Then, a little later, in the year 70, Jerusalem and the land of Judah would be devastated by the Roman armies. Christians in Jerusalem and the surrounding area, obeying Christ's warning, would flee out of Judea prior to the city's destruction, saving their lives, but losing their possessions and facing many hardships.

So James' letter was timely for those circumstances. But whether under heavy persecution or not, Christians have need of endurance. For they cannot escape living in a world that flouts Christian principles. In addition, they have to deal with human frailties, with sickness and many other problems. James' words on endurance, explaining how God gives the Christian wisdom to endure, are vital to Christian life.

Though The Letter of James was one of the last books of the Christian Scriptures to be acknowledged as canonical, there can be no doubt as to its being an integral part of the inspired written Word of God, tied in closely with the rest of the Scriptures and with Christ's own personal teachings. James quotes or refers to the Hebrew Scriptures with regard to: man's creation (Jas. 3:9; Gen. 1:26); Abraham and Rahab (Jas. 2:21-25; Gen. 15:6; 22:9-12; Josh. chap. 2; Isa. 41:8); Job (Jas. 5:11; Job 1:13-22; 2:7-10; 42:10-17); the Law (Jas. 2:8, 10, 11; Ex. 20:13, 14; Lev. 19:18; Deut. 5:17, 18); and Elijah (Jas. 5:17, 18; 1 Ki. 17:1; 18:1). There are many pointed examples of direct harmony with statements of Jesus Christ. To name a few: concerning persecution (Jas. 1:2; Matt. 5:10-12); asking for and receiving things from God (Jas. 1:5, 17; Luke 11:9-13); being both hearers and doers (Jas. 1:22; Matt. 7:21-27); separateness from the world (Jas. 4:4; John 17:14); not judging others (Jas. 4:12; Luke 6:37); reliability of one's word. —Jas. 5:12; Matt. 5:33-37.

Moreover, James' letter has a strong prophetic tone and contains many figures and similes, giving it a certain resemblance to Jesus Christ's discourses, such as the Sermon on the Mount. Like his half brother Jesus, James drew on physical things—the sea, vegetation, animals, boats, a farmer, the earth—to give colorful backing to his arguments on faith, control of the tongue, patience, and so forth. (Jas. 1:6, 9-11; 3:3-12; 5:7) This, together with the use of pointed questions and more than 50 imperatives in this relatively short letter, makes James' letter one full of moving power.

The Bible would not be complete without The Letter of James, for it emphasizes essential elements of the Christian's advancement toward holiness and a closer relationship to God and Christ, and to fellow Christians. It helps him to make his worship of God a reality that can be observed by all, and of practical and upbuilding value to himself and others. This harmonizes with Jesus' words: "Let your light shine before men, that they may see your fine works and give glory to your Father who is in the heavens."—Matt. 5:16.

Consequently, the reader can get much needed comfort from reading the letter, besides a great deal of encouragement and guidance in applying Christian principles to his everyday life, with hope in God's help now and in the everlasting salvation that he holds out for those who love him. We trust that the reader of The Letter of James and the commentary to follow will take time to meditate on the things read. For, unless this is done, the study will be primarily intellectual but barren of fruitage, for the truths expressed are deep, affecting the heart.—Heb. 4:12.

Commentary
on The Letter of James

CHAPTER 1

1 James, a slave of God and of the Lord Jesus Christ, to the twelve tribes that are scattered about: Greetings!

---

1 James

The Christian Greek Scriptures mention four persons by this name: (1) The father of the faithful apostle Judas. (Luke 6:16; Acts 1:13) (2) The brother of the apostle John. (Matt. 10:2) (3) The apostle who was the son of Alphaeus. (Matt. 10:3) (4) The son of Joseph and Mary and half brother of Jesus. (Mark 6:3; Gal. 1:19) The writer of The Letter of James was evidently not the father of the apostle Judas (not Iscariot), as there is no record that Judas' father even became a disciple of the Lord Jesus Christ or was alive at this time. The brother of the apostle John is ruled out, since he was executed in the early days of the Christian congregation, about 44 C.E. (Acts 12:1, 2) Since the writer of the letter did not refer to himself as an apostle, evidently he was not the son of Alphaeus. This leaves only James, the half brother of Jesus, as the writer of this letter. It is noteworthy that Jude (Judas), also a half brother of Jesus, identifies himself as "a brother of James," and in his letter refers

Salutation

11

to the apostles as "they," excluding himself. (Jude 1, 17, 18) This provides additional confirmation that the writer James was not one of the 12 apostles, but "the brother of the Lord."—Gal. 1:19; Mark 6:3.

a slave of God and of the Lord Jesus Christ

Like his brother Jude, James does not capitalize on his fleshly relationship with the Son of God but humbly refers to himself as a mere servant or slave of God and of his Lord, Master or Owner Jesus Christ. (Jude 1) With his precious blood, Jesus Christ has purchased his followers and is, therefore, their Owner. (1 Cor. 7:23; 2 Pet. 2:1; Jude 4) He is their King and Bridegroom to whom they are subject as their Lord. (Col. 1:13; Eph. 5:22-24) Nevertheless, though Jesus Christ is his Lord, the Christian is also a slave of God. James properly begins his letter acknowledging his accountability to Jehovah God and to Jesus Christ, for as a slave to both he was under obligation to carry out what they required of him.

to the twelve tribes

These are not the 12 tribes of literal Israel, as those tribes of natural Israelites were not the "brothers" of James who were "holding the faith of our Lord Jesus Christ." (Compare James 1:2; 2:1, 5.) While on earth, Jesus Christ had indicated that the Jews as a national entity would be rejected. He said that 'the kingdom of God would be taken away from them and be given to a nation producing its fruits.' (Matt. 21:43) That "nation" proved to be spiritual Israel, the real "Israel of God," composed of Christianized Jews and believing non-Jews. (Gal. 6:16) Since natural Israel consisted of 12 tribes, it logically follows that spiritual Israel would be spoken of as having 12 tribes to show that it was a complete spiritual nation, with no part or tribe missing. There is no numerical imbalance within spiritual Israel, for the Bible book of Revelation symbolically reveals that an equal number—12,000—is sealed from every tribe. (Rev. 7:4-8) A member of this spiritual Israel must have the circumcision of the heart and a faith like that of Abraham. This is what makes a real Israelite or Jew. (Rom. 2:29; 4:16, 17; 9:6-8; Gal. 3:7, 29; 4:21-31; Phil. 3:3)

that are scattered about

Spiritual Israelites were dispersed throughout the then known world. Initially, after persecution broke out against the Jerusalem congregation, the disciples, with the exception of the apostles, were scattered. (Acts 8:1) In time, through the activity of the scattered disciples and that of evangelizers, congregations sprang up in many areas. That is why Peter could use the same phrase as did James, writing "to the temporary residents scattered about in Pontus, Galatia, Cappadocia, Asia, and Bithynia, to the ones chosen." (1 Pet. 1:1)

Greetings!

Literally, the Greek expression here means "to be rejoicing," the absolute infinitive of the verb in the sense of an imperative. This salutation, in effect, expressed the thought "May you have joy" or "May things be well with you." It commonly appears in extant non-Biblical papyrus letters. Also, the military commander Claudius Lysias used the expression in his letter to Governor Felix. (Acts 23:26) The Greek term does not appear as a salutation in any of the Bible letters of the apostles. (The apostle John did write about saying a "greeting," using the same infinitive form, "to be rejoicing." [2 John 10, 11]) It may be noted that the letter setting forth the decision on circumcision contained this salutation. (Acts 15:23) Since the disciple James suggested the

2 Consider it all joy, my brothers, when you
meet with various trials,

---

formulation of that letter, additional support is
provided for the conclusion that the James who
wrote the letter bearing his name is the same one
who had a prominent part in the deliberations
recounted at Acts chapter 15.

2 Consider it all joy

Having given greetings, James proceeds to dis-
cuss a vital subject, the proper reaction of Christians to trials. Instead of viewing
Seeking   trials with feelings of self-pity,
                     sadness, depression or fear, Chris-
Wisdom for   tians are encouraged to regard
Endurance   them as a reason for rejoicing. This
                     does not ignore the fact that trials
can be very "grievous." In itself, the affliction
gives no reason to feel elated, for it may be very
painful. (Heb. 12:11) However, James is looking
at the matter of trials from the standpoint of what
the final result can be. Hence, while undergoing
trial, we should consider the situation all joy,
realizing that the experience can be for our good,
our lasting happiness. (Matt. 5:10-12)

my brothers

The Christian congregation is an "association
of brothers," its members being spiritual brothers.
(1 Pet. 2:17; 5:9) Jesus Christ told his disciples:
"All you are brothers." (Matt. 23:8) By addressing fellow believers as "my brothers," James acknowledged that he was on the same level with
them. As a brother, he was vitally interested in
them, concerned about the trials that were be-
falling them and desirous of their heeding his
counsel as coming from a beloved brother.

3 knowing as you do that this tested quality of your faith works out endurance.

---

when you meet with various trials

As Christians we encounter many trials. The Greek term for "meet with" implies an unexpected and an unwelcome encounter, as when a person comes face to face with a robber. (Luke 10:30, where the same verb is rendered "fell among") The trials, adversities, difficulties or afflictions may include those that are common to humans generally—sickness, poverty, loss of loved ones, temptations and other trialsome things for our faith. Additionally, we must expect suffering for being slaves of Jehovah God and of the Lord Jesus Christ. (1 Pet. 2:19–3:1) The apostle Paul wrote: "All those desiring to live with godly devotion in association with Christ Jesus will also be persecuted." (2 Tim. 3:12) Paul told Christians at Thessalonica that they were "destined to suffer tribulation." (1 Thess. 3:3, 4)

3 knowing as you do that this tested quality of your faith works out endurance

This phrase explains why we can regard undergoing trials as "all joy." It is because of knowing, realizing or being aware of the fact that trials can benefit us. (1 Pet. 1:6, 7) The expression "tested quality" literally means "proof" or "approved part" or "that which is approved" or "tried or approved quality." Through trials, our faith becomes one of tested quality. It becomes a proved or tried faith that has successfully undergone a period of difficulty. By having our faith tested by trials, we are enabled to develop strength for endurance, not a mere toleration of distressing things, but endurance with steadfastness, con-

4 But let endurance have its work complete, that
you may be complete and sound in all respects,
not lacking in anything.

---

stancy and integrity in the face of temptation
and affliction.

4 But let endurance have its work complete

This is encouragement for us to submit humbly
to our afflictions. We need to recognize *why* afflictions must come, and the reason for steadfast
endurance. We should not respond to trials by
murmuring and complaining or by giving in to
fear or weariness. There may be temptation to
escape the trial by an unscriptural course. But
we must guard against interrupting in such a
way the beneficial work that our faithful endurance under trial is accomplishing. For as long as
God allows the trial to continue, endurance should
be permitted to do its beneficial work to comple-
tion. Jesus said: "By endurance on your part
you will acquire your souls," or win your lives.
(Luke 21:19)

**that you may be complete and sound in all
respects, not lacking in anything**

The "work" that endurance is performing will
make us complete or whole as Christians. By enduring faithfully, we have our faith refined. The
difficult experience that we undergo may teach
us how to be more reasonable, sympathetic and
compassionate in dealing with others. Also, areas
wherein the stress of the trial may show up weaknesses can thereafter be strengthened. After passing through one trial successfully, we are in a
better position to face up to any future bad circumstance that may arise. As a result of this, we
will not be lacking or defective in faith or in
any of the other qualities that we should have

5 So, if any one of you is lacking in wisdom, let him keep on asking God, for he gives generously to all and without reproaching; and it will be given him.

---

as Christians. We will become better servants of God by allowing the trial to mold us in a favorable way. The goal is to "be perfect [complete], as your heavenly Father is perfect." (Matt. 5:48)

5 So, if any one of you is lacking in wisdom

Wisdom involves sound judgment, based on knowledge and understanding. It is the ability to apply knowledge and understanding successfully in solving problems, avoiding dangers or attaining certain goals. The wisdom that Christians ask for is wisdom for living so as to please God in all features of their lives, especially in facing trials. How might lack of wisdom in the face of trials manifest itself? We may not know just what to do in dealing with a trialsome situation. Or, we may not have a clear view as to how God's permission of the bitter experience can benefit us. Instead of looking at the matter from Jehovah's standpoint, we may react according to imperfect human feelings or sensations. (Compare Psalm 73:21, 22.)

let him keep on asking God

We should earnestly pray for wisdom. It is not enough just to do so once. But we should *persevere* in prayer when undergoing trials. This persistence is evidence to God of our real, deep concern, not a mere passing wish or matter of indifference. By praying only once or twice over an important matter, we might be doing it as a duty or as a matter of routine or ritual. By so praying we may be giving evidence that we do not put much faith in getting an answer. (Matt. 7:7-11; Luke 11:5-13; Rom. 12:12)

for he gives generously to all and without reproaching

To all who approach him in faith, Jehovah God gives generously, without any restraint or reservation. He has no ulterior motives, but is wholehearted in his giving. Moreover, Jehovah God will not make us feel stupid or foolish for approaching him in prayer. He does not react as do men, who say: 'Why, you should know better than that.' 'That is a childish request.' 'How can you be so stupid as to think in such a way?' 'You have come to me repeatedly with such problems, and I have tried to help you. But this is just too much.' No, regardless of how often we approach the Most High for wisdom and no matter how minor the problem may be, he will not reproach, shame or chide us. He does not humiliate us by calling to our attention our past failures, as humans are prone to do. He deeply appreciates the person who has the faith and the concern to pray repeatedly for a certain thing. (Luke 18:1-8)

and it will be given him

Jehovah God will not withhold from us the needed wisdom to take the proper view of a trial and to put up with it and deal with it successfully. This does not mean that the problem will always go away or be worked out immediately, but that we will be able to take the course that will do good, spiritually, for us and for others concerned. We will endure the trial successfully to the end and will come through it better Christians than we were when we went into it. And others who observe us, and who have a right heart, will be helped, strengthened by our example.

There are many other things over which we may pray and that may not be answered in the

6 But let him keep on asking in faith, not doubting at all, for he who doubts is like a wave of the sea driven by the wind and blown about.

---

way that we might personally desire. We will get an answer, possibly different from what we expect; it will be what God knows is best for us. In fact, some things that we ask for might not be for our benefit if they were granted as we ask or desire. However, *wisdom* to face a trial is absolutely promised by God. We are sure to get the necessary wisdom if we ask properly. The wisdom will be given in one or more of several ways. For example: (1) Certain Scripture passages that provide the answer that we need will be called to our attention under guidance of God's spirit, either through our own study or meditation or through our brothers. (Gal. 5:25; Eph. 1:17) (2) Circumstances and events as maneuvered through God's providence will enable us to see clearly what to do. Certain obstacles may be removed from our path. (3) The holy angels serve God by helping his people, and they may share in directing us to the right course. (Heb. 1:14) Jesus said: "If you, although being wicked, know how to give good gifts to your children, how much more so will the Father in heaven give holy spirit to those asking him!" (Luke 11:13)

6 But let him keep on asking in faith, not doubting at all

Our appeal to God for wisdom in connection with trials should be made in faith. It is the kind of faith, trust or confidence that one should have toward a loving father who is deeply interested in the welfare of his children. There should not be even the slightest doubt about our needing wisdom and about God's granting it. The petitioner must have full faith in God and his Son, and in their readiness to provide what is needed. He must have no motive other than the interests of the Christian faith and the purposes of God. His own personal welfare is, of course, tied closely to these things, and such a prayer will be in his own best interests also. (Mark 11:24)

for he who doubts is like a wave of the sea driven by the wind and blown about

The person who is unsure about his petitions, as to whether God will answer them, is indeed unstable. The uncertainty robs him of his peace of mind and heart. He may at times experience a surge of hope and trust, and then lapse into despair

and doubt. He does not wholeheartedly commit all his affairs to Jehovah God. Such a doubter is like a wave of the sea, tossed about in every direction —up and down as well as sideways. Because he lacks firm conviction, he is easily influenced by the pressure of circumstances. (Compare Ephesians 4:14.)

7 In fact, let not that man suppose that he will receive anything from Jehovah; **8** he is an indecisive man, unsteady in all his ways.

9 But let the lowly brother exult over his exaltation,

---

7 In fact, let not that man suppose that he will receive anything from Jehovah

Surely, when a person prays and at the same time feels doubtful in his heart, he should not expect to receive anything from Jehovah. He does not wholeheartedly expect divine help. His doubts prevent him from putting his full trust in the Most High, leaning on him. He does not have the faith that God requires, because "without faith it is impossible to please him well, for he that approaches God must believe that he is and that he becomes the rewarder of those earnestly seeking him." (Heb. 11:6)

8 he is an indecisive man, unsteady in all his ways

His doubting, his lack of trust, is not limited to matters involving prayer. The same doubting spirit is manifest in all other aspects of his life. Because of his indecisiveness, he wobbles "in all his ways." He does not adhere to anything. Such indecision would make divine guidance of virtually no value, since the indecisive one would not be likely to follow through and act on it. In his unsteadiness, he is not actually settled in his own mind as to what he really wants to do, even as to being genuinely determined to follow what guidance God might give.

9 But let the lowly brother exult over his exaltation

Most of the Christians were, and are today,

10 and the rich one over his humiliation, because
like a flower of the vegetation he will pass away.

---

people of humble birth. (1 Cor. 1:26) Prior to
their becoming disciples of Jesus Christ, they had
little as to material wealth.
Cause for Rich (Jas. 2:5) In the world such
and people are generally looked
Poor to Exult down on, even despised. But on
coming to an accurate knowl-
edge of the truth, they are ex-
alted, elevated to the dignified standing of Kingdom heirs with Jesus Christ. (Rom. 8:17)

Also, some in the congregation had been rich
but were made poor by persecution. (Heb. 10:32-
34) These all realized that they had gained the
precious possession of an approved relationship
with God and Christ, and the prospect of everlasting life. In the congregation, those who are
poor enjoy the unqualified standing of brothers
and sisters along with all the other members.
Their lowly economic state is of no spiritual dis-
advantage. Distinctions according to position or
wealth have no place in the Christian congregation. With the depository of spiritual riches, poor
ones are as effective as rich ones in aiding others
to follow the course that leads to eternal life.
(2 Cor. 6:10; 8:9; Gal. 3:28, 29; 1 Pet. 4:10, 11;
Rev. 2:9; see comments on James 2:1-9.)

10 and the rich one over his humiliation

On coming to a knowledge of the truth, the
rich person is taught that what he once trusted
in—his wealth—is transitory. He now discerns
clearly "the deceptive power of riches." (Matt.
13:22) This results in a humiliation for him, as

he is helped to see himself and his possessions in the right perspective. He realizes that spending time and effort in the avid pursuit of riches is a waste and tends to destroy spirituality and, often, physical health. (1 Tim. 6:9, 10) Compared with the lasting spiritual riches, material possessions and high standing in the world amount to nothing. (Compare Philippians 3:8.)

Rather than high-mindedness, which riches often produce, the spirit of Christ is one of lowliness and humility. (Phil. 2:3-8) It may also be noted

that, in the world, the rich person is held in high esteem. However, when he becomes a true disciple of Jesus Christ, others may begin to look down on him. (Compare John 7:47-52; 12:42, 43.) Because of possessing the more valuable spiritual riches, the individual has much reason to rejoice over his humiliation.

because like a flower of the vegetation he will pass away

A flower may be very beautiful, resembling the rich man in his splendid clothing and with his fine possessions. But the flower wilts and dries up.

> **11** For the sun rises with its burning heat and withers the vegetation, and its flower drops off and the beauty of its outward appearance perishes. So, too, the rich man will fade away in his ways of life.

Likewise, the rich man cannot keep himself alive indefinitely. He, too, will pass away in death. Riches are of no value in lengthening a limited life-span. (Compare Psalm 49:6-9; Matthew 6:27.)

11 For the sun rises with its burning heat and withers the vegetation, and its flower drops off and the beauty of its outward appearance perishes

No matter how luxuriant vegetation may be, let a dry spell come and the sun's fierce heat quickly causes the vegetation to wither. Flowers that looked so beautiful fade, droop and fall from the stem; the once attractive plant has lost its beauty.

So, too, the rich man will fade away in his ways of life

Unlike the poor man whose outward appearance is not impressive, the rich man resembles a beautiful flower, as he is bedecked with finery. However, while pursuing his ways, perhaps traveling on some business venture or during his daily routine in seeking more wealth, or while enjoying the luxury that his riches afford, he dies. Since he cannot take his glory and riches with him to the grave, he loses his attractive outward appearance. He may not even have had time to enjoy his riches.

On the other hand, the rich man who becomes a Christian can genuinely enjoy his material wealth because of using it to promote the interests of Christianity and to spread the good news of the Kingdom. (1 Tim. 6:17-19) He can help the needy, especially giving attention to his Christian brothers, as the early congregation did. (Acts 4:32-37; Jas. 1:27)

Of course, the poor man also dies, but he never presented the beautiful blossoming appearance of the rich man, whose wealth would seem capable of giving him advantages that could extend his life. The psalmist David described those trusting and exulting in material wealth as saying: "Our garners [are] full, furnishing products of one sort after another, our flocks multiplying by thousands, ten thousand to one, in our streets, our cattle loaded down, without any rupture and with no abortion . . . Happy is the people for whom it is just like that!" But David goes on to say, instead: "Happy is the people whose God is Jehovah!" (Ps. 144:13-15)

Jesus also illustrated this point by describing the rich man who exulted altogether in his riches: "The land of a certain rich man produced well. Consequently he began reasoning within himself, saying, 'What shall I do, now that I have nowhere to gather my crops?' So he said, 'I will do this: I will tear down my storehouses and build bigger ones, and there I will gather all my grain and all my good things; and I will say to my soul: "Soul, you have many good things laid up for many years; take your ease, eat, drink, enjoy yourself." ' But God said to him, 'Unreasonable one, this night they are demanding your soul from you. Who, then, is to have the things you stored up?' So it goes with the man that lays up treasure for himself but is not rich toward God." (Luke 12:16-21)

12 Happy is the man that keeps on enduring trial, because on becoming approved he will receive the crown of life, which Jehovah promised to those who continue loving him.

---

12 Happy is the man that keeps on enduring trial

James here refers to trials from outside, not inward temptation, for, as one Bible scholar notes:

Happiness to Those Enduring
"Inner enticement to evil would have to be resisted, not endured."* Not that trials cannot also bring about or contribute to temptations to do wrong. (Compare Matthew 16:21-23.) But James is focusing on *enduring* trials. By contrast, any incitement or pressure to do wrong that rises within us should be speedily dismissed. The man who does not give up when faced with a trialsome situation but who keeps on enduring faithfully is the one who can be pronounced happy. There is real joy and satisfaction in knowing that we are preserving a clean conscience and doing what is right despite difficulties, trials or temptations that could make us deviate from what is upright. We feel a closeness to our Creator as we continue to experience his loving care in time of adversity. (1 Pet. 5:7)

because on becoming approved he will receive the crown of life

Faithful endurance results in more than present happiness. By remaining an approved servant of Jehovah, the spirit-begotten Christian is sure to receive the "crown of life." This does not mean that he earns the right to life by his endurance of trials, but he is honored as with a "crown" by

---

* *The International Critical Commentary*, on The Letter of James, by Professor J. H. Ropes, p. 150.

13 When under trial, let no one say: "I am being tried by God." For with evil things God cannot be tried nor does he himself try anyone.

---

the gift of heavenly life. Life cannot be *earned* by imperfect humans but is the free *gift* through faith in Jesus Christ. (Rom. 6:23) The *enduring* Christian has proved that he has that faith. Its quality has been tested and found complete.

which Jehovah promised to those who continue loving him

The "crown" (life itself) is promised to all spirit-begotten Christians who continue loving Jehovah, who prove to be his real friends. This love is shown by obedience to God's commands. (1 John 5:3; contrast with Romans 1:28-32.) God, through Christ, causes the Christian's trials to work together to perfect his servants, if they endure these steadfastly, uncomplainingly and, with his help, triumphantly down till death. (Rom. 8:28; 1 Pet. 5:10)

13 When under trial, let no one say: "I am being tried by God"

When experiencing any kind of affliction or adversity, a person would be wrong in concluding that Jehovah God is trying to induce him to commit sin. If the individual lets something in connection with the trial become a temptation to him—for example, if he turns from resistance to yielding because of some selfish advantage, or because he is seeking a way to avoid facing and enduring the trial—God is not to blame. For God will give strength to endure if the Christian remains steadfast in his own heart. (Phil. 4:13) The divine

How Sin Takes Place in Humans

14 But each one is tried by being drawn out and enticed by his own desire.

---

arrangement, God's way of dealing with his servants, never leads to sin. Whatever God permits to befall us is in no way designed to cause us to transgress or to make wrongdoing look attractive.

For with evil things God cannot be tried

Jehovah God is holy, pure, clean. He cannot be induced by any kind of evil or any undesirable situation or circumstance to commit wrong. There is no way in which to make wrong things attractive to the Most High, trying him with them.

nor does he himself try anyone

Just as Jehovah cannot be led into sin, so he does not put things before us to encourage us to violate his commands, or to weaken our resistance to wrongdoing. He does not place us in a situation where something that we definitely need can be obtained only by breaking his law. Though God permits trials to come, he does not try his servants with evil intent. He seeks our good, our betterment, never our harm. Satan, however, may use the trial as a temptation to the individual to do wrong. But, for the faithful Christian, God prevails over Satan's efforts and uses the trial as a disciplining and perfecting agency, so that the Christian is blessed by it. (Heb. 12:7, 11)

14 But each one is tried by being drawn out and enticed by his own desire

Circumstances may bring a trial on a person. But the real test, that which induces one to sin, resides in the sinful human. The Christian, therefore, must guard his heart. The Scriptures say: "The heart is more treacherous than anything else and is desperate. Who can know it?" (Jer.

17:9) This kind of trial, that is, the pressure to sin, bears down on the human weakness, and the real danger exists in an individual's inner reaction to the circumstances. A particular situation may give rise to a wrong desire. This desire then serves as an inducement to commit sin. The person is thereby bringing himself into temptation. (Compare Matthew 26:41.) To illustrate: A Christian may be physically abused, even tortured, because of his faith. The purpose of the persecution is to break his integrity. This unpleasant circumstance may suggest to the Christian that he could escape further mistreatment and possibly even death by compromising. If the desire for relief continues to build up, he may choose to get out of the trialsome situation by breaking his integrity. The Christian who gives in to any wrong desire cannot excuse himself and blame God or anyone else. In the final analysis, he himself has let his own inward desire overcome him, when he could have resisted, just as Jesus did, and would have received God's help. (Matt. 4:1-11)

Satan and the world under his influence try people with evil things or with evil intent. (2 Cor. 4:4; John 14:30) The world uses (1) the desire of the flesh, which is fallen, imperfect; (2) the desire of the eyes, with greediness; (3) the showy display of one's means of life, a parading of glory, position, power, prominence, and so forth. (1 John 2:16) These things did not appeal at all to Jesus, because he saw how worthless they are; and he had no tendency to sin and no principle of evil in him to be incited by the temptation. (Matt. 4:4-10)

A Christian, therefore, is tried in this evil way only when he lets the imperfection, the evil in the members of his fallen flesh, become excited. If he does this, the sin finally gets mastery over him, as James goes on to show; and it controls

15 Then the desire, when it has become fertile, gives birth to sin; in turn, sin, when it has been accomplished, brings forth death.

---

his actions. (Compare Romans 6:14, 19.) This he would bring about by failing to dismiss immediately the evil presentation or thought from his mind. That is why we pray: "Do not bring us into temptation." (Matt. 6:13) We ask God to guard our minds and hearts so that we will immediately discern the badness, rejecting it promptly. That is why we need constantly to study the Bible, its warnings and safeguards, keeping our minds on the worthwhile things. (Phil. 4:8)

The night before his death, Jesus said: "The ruler of the world is coming [to kill me]. And he has no hold on me [or, nothing "in me." (*Kingdom Interlinear Translation*)]." (John 14:30) Satan and Jesus had nothing in common. There was no principle of evil, no imperfection, no tendency to cater to wrong desires of the flesh in Jesus. There was no sinful weakness in Jesus that Satan could play on, as he can with imperfect men. (Heb. 2:14, 15) The things Jesus underwent that night and the next day constituted a trial. (Heb. 2:18; 5:7, 8) Yet to Jesus it was not a trial able to induce him to do evil or to bring him to do wrong, for Jesus would not for a second entertain any compromise, violation of integrity or the doing of anything having a shade of wrong. He could not be turned aside from undergoing that which the Father had allowed to come upon him.

15 Then the desire, when it has become fertile, gives birth to sin

When we entertain a wrong desire instead of dismissing it, we allow it to become fertile. Like a planted seed, it has the potential for growth.

James 1:16

16 Do not be misled, my beloved brothers.

Then, when we ourselves, by entertaining the idea, supply cultivation, it is sure to sprout. By the desire's being nurtured in the heart, the individual eventually commits sin. Thus an act of sin is the ~~ing of a wrong desire that is nourished to~~ mean to say that Psalm 7:14.) James does not until it breaks forth in a wrongful act, for the nurturing of the wrong desire is in itself sinful. For example, the apostle John wrote: "Everyone who hates his brother is a manslayer, and you know that no manslayer has everlasting life remaining in him." (1 John 3:15; compare Matthew 5:28.) The wrong desire is parent to the wrong act, finds its expression in it; and it is to that manifestation of sin that James refers.

in turn, sin, when it has been accomplished, brings forth death

It is a sobering thought that *any* sin can lead to death. If any wrong desire is allowed to take root in a person's heart and God's law is violated, the individual comes under condemnation. If not corrected, he may even come under mastery by the sin and the related wrongdoing, and deserve death. "The wages sin pays is death." (Rom. 6:23) This certainly emphasizes the importance of resisting the sinful inclinations of the flesh.

16 Do not be misled

James did not want fellow Christians to be misled into thinking that Jehovah God was the source of their trials. Such a view would misrepresent the Most High, as it would associate him with evil and make him the cause of sin. Nor can the Christian make the excuse that the temptation

God's Gifts

17 Every good gift and every perfect present is from above, for it comes down from the Father of the celestial lights, and with him there is not a variation of the turning of the shadow.

---

he experiences is greater than he can bear, for the Scriptures assure us: "God is faithful, and he will not let you be tempted beyond what you can bear, but along with the temptation to be able also make the way out." (1 Cor. 10:13) It would be detrimental to the Christian to believe that God was bringing such pressure on him and such view could cause him, wrongly, to take offense against Jehovah God.

my beloved brothers

Even though his fellow believers were imperfect and failed in many respects, James assumes no superiority but, instead, recognizes them as his brothers, for whom he has affection. By here addressing them as "my beloved brothers," he evidently also seeks to stimulate their attention and direct it to the important point that he is now making.

17 Every good gift and every perfect present is from above

The gifts that humans give do not always turn out to be good for all concerned, and often the motive in giving is not pure; hence, there is imperfection in human gifts. This does not mean that no human gift is good. In fact, at times gifts from God come by human instrumentality. Jehovah God is the *source* of anything that is *altogether good in every respect*. Only perfect gifts come from him. "He himself gives to all persons life and breath and all things." (Acts 17:25) God's giving is invariably pure and promotes the welfare and happiness of humankind. (Acts 14: 17) He furnishes us all things "richly for our enjoyment." (1 Tim. 6:17) Also, God's gifts are complete, flawless. There is nothing lacking in them. Because Jehovah dwells in the highest heavens, "every good gift and every perfect present" can be spoken of as coming "from above," that is, from his place of residence.

for it comes down from the Father of the celestial lights

"Every good gift and every perfect present" originates with the Father or the Creator of the "celestial lights"—the sun, the moon and the stars. He speaks of himself as "the Giver of the sun for light by day, the statutes of the moon and the stars for light by night, the One stirring up the sea that its waves may become boisterous, the One whose name is Jehovah of armies." (Jer. 31:35) However, he is not just the Maker of the heavenly bodies; he is also the source of spiritual enlightenment. The apostle Paul writes: "For God is he who said: 'Let the light shine out of darkness,' and he has shone on our hearts to illuminate them with the glorious knowledge of God by the face of Christ." (2 Cor. 4:6)

and with him there is not a variation of the turning of the shadow

In its rising and setting, the sun casts shadows of changing length and intensity. Depending on the position of the earth in its rotation and in its orbit, considerable variation occurs in the way that the sun's radiant heat and light are distributed. Unlike the sun, the Creator of the heavenly bodies is not subject to changes. There is no variation with him, as when the sun causes a change in shadows by a change in its position in the sky. Only at high noon is the sun at its zenith with

18 Because he willed it, he brought us forth by the word of truth, for us to be certain firstfruits of his creatures.

---

reference to the observer. Jehovah God, however, always is at his zenith in providing what is good. We can always rely on him.

18 Because he willed it, he brought us forth by the word of truth

It is according to God's will, operating to bring about his good purpose, that individuals are brought forth as spiritual sons. In harmony with his preceding words, James is showing that one of the *very finest* gifts—spiritual birth—is from God, and that his will always works good. This is in contrast with sin, which brings forth death. God has no part whatever in causing us to sin. God's spiritual sons are brought forth by God's spirit, or active force, working in conjunction with the word of truth, the message of "good news." The apostle Paul says of this: "By means of [Christ] also, after you believed, you were sealed with the promised holy spirit, which is a token in advance of our inheritance, for the purpose of releasing by a ransom God's own possession, to his glorious praise." (Eph. 1:13, 14)

for us to be certain firstfruits of his creatures

God's purpose respecting those who are begotten by his spirit is for them to be a "certain firstfruits," or, 'a kind of firstfruits.' They are taken out from among mankind as a firstfruits to God. According to the Law given to Israel, the firstfruits were offered to the Most High. (Ex. 22:29, 30; 23:19) Ancient Israel was called "the first yield" to God. (Jer. 2:3) Likewise, those taken out from among mankind are set apart for sacred service, to be "a kingdom and priests" to

> **19** Know this, my beloved brothers. Every man must be swift about hearing, slow about speaking, slow about wrath;

God. (Rev. 5:10) James may also have had in mind the offering of the barley firstfruits on Nisan 16 (which, in 33 C.E., was the day of Jesus' resurrection) and the offering of the two loaves of wheat on Pentecost day (the occasion of the outpouring of holy spirit). (Lev. 23:4-11, 15-17) With this in view, Christ himself would be *the* firstfruits; his joint heirs, "certain" firstfruits.

19 Know this, my beloved brothers

The words "know this" may refer back to the fact that, as Christians, they had been brought forth to be "certain firstfruits." Their really *knowing* this would reflect itself in action. Jesus said to his faithful apostles: "If you know these things, happy you are if you do them." (John 13:17) Of a righteous man (King Josiah), the prophet Jeremiah said: "He pleaded the legal claim of the afflicted one and the poor one. In that case it went well. 'Was not that a case of *knowing* me?' is the utterance of Jehovah." (Jer. 22:16) This righteous man acted on that which he really and truly *knew* about Jehovah God in his heart. (Compare 1 John 3:6.) Again the disciple James wants to call the attention of fellow believers to an important point and so addresses them as "my beloved brothers." He says, in effect: 'Knowing that God has given you a new birth by the word of truth, you should, being so greatly honored, reflect this newness of life in your conduct, living up to that for which you were called,' as next indicated.

Hearing and Doing

Every man must be swift about hearing

Surely Christians should be quick to respond to God's word or message. Hearing, in this case, also has the sense of obeying. (John 8:37, 38, 47) We should be not only hearers, but doers also. All pride, stubbornness, prejudice and personal opinion should be laid aside in the meek hearing of God's "word." We should desire God's "word" just as an infant desires milk. Not that we are all babes, spiritually, but that we *long* for the word just as babes eagerly look for their feeding of milk. (Compare 1 Peter 2:2.) The similarity is not in being babes, but in having a strong, anxious desire to feed constantly on that word.

slow about speaking

Before speaking, we should give thoughtful consideration to what we are going to say. (Prov. 15:28; 16:23) Not until we ourselves have paid attention to God's requirements are we in a position to teach others. (Rom. 2:17-24) We must guard against becoming like those described by the apostle Paul as men who wanted to be teachers but did not understand the words that they were using nor the concepts 'about which they were making strong assertions.' (1 Tim. 1:7) We should not be talking, giving out ideas to others, until we have first listened carefully to what God's Word has to say. If we do not have Bible backing for what we say, we can greatly mislead ourselves and others. Proverbs 17:27 states: "Anyone holding back his sayings is possessed of knowledge, and a man of discernment is cool of spirit."

James' counsel about being slow to speak is seen to be timely, in view of the correction he was constrained to give the brothers in chapters 3 and 4 of his letter.

20 for man's wrath does not work out God's righteousness.

---

slow about wrath

We are admonished to work hard to keep anger in check, not allowing ourselves to lose our temper. Since this point is made in connection with obedient response to the "word" of truth, manifestly any examination of the truth must be approached with the right frame of mind and heart. While in an agitated state, a person cannot really appreciate divine requirements. (Compare Proverbs 19:3.) He is in no condition to act in harmony with them. If we are angered by what others say, we should 'slow down' before answering, so as to avoid a bitter, vindictive reply, which may anger and alienate others and cause us great trouble. Sometimes we may be angry, but then the Bible warns: "Be wrathful, and yet do not sin." (Eph. 4:26) At such a point, being slow about expressing anger will save us from sinning.

20 for man's wrath does not work out God's righteousness

The righteousness that God requires his servants to display can never spring from a wrathful disposition. Wrath will not motivate a person to obey the Scriptures. In an angry state, the individual is far more likely to do something that he will later regret, perhaps all his lifetime. Man's wrath also obscures God's righteousness. When others see one who claims to serve God but who is prone to wrathful actions, they cannot see in the professed Christian a true likeness of God. They may question the desirability of serving a God whose servants display such a bad quality. Therefore, when those claiming to be his servants are wrathful, they put an obstacle in the way of

21 Hence put away all filthiness and that superfluous thing, badness, and accept with mildness
the implanting of the word which is able to save
your souls.

---

others' accepting the truth. It may prejudice persons so that they will turn a deaf ear to Bible
truth that the Christian and his associates are
proclaiming. The Proverb says: "He that is slow
to anger is abundant in discernment, but one that
is impatient is exalting foolishness." (Prov. 14:29)

21 Hence put away all filthiness

In view of the fact that the Christian should
want to be swift about hearing, slow about speaking and slow about wrath, he should rid himself
of all filthiness, that is, all things that are dis-
gusting or offensive from Jehovah's standpoint.
These things promote in us disobedience and
wrathfulness. Filthiness in attitudes and actions
are included. Sin has a "deceptive power" that
can make it look appealing, desirable, attractive
to us. (Heb. 3:13) We need to see it in its true
light, recognizing its repugnant nature—the way
it fouls up people's lives, degrades them, leaves
ugly stains on their names and in their minds
and hearts. (Compare Jude 23.) A healthy hatred
of wrongdoing is a great protection against it.
The Christian must have a pure mind and heart
in order to come fully under the wholesome influence of the word of truth.

and that superfluous thing, badness

The Greek word used by James, here rendered
"superfluous," has the basic sense of "abundant,"
and can also mean "excessive," including that
which remains as a surplus. (Compare the use of
forms of this term at Matthew 5:37; 14:20.) Thus
some translations read: "the evil that is so prev-

alent" (*New International Version*); "rank growth of wickedness" (*Revised Standard Version*). All badness is undesirable, and, like leaven, seeks to expand and grow in us. (1 Cor. 5:6) Evidently, therefore, the "superfluous thing, badness," refers to any kind of badness, baseness, that keeps cropping up in the heart. (Compare Romans 7: 13-25.) This is because our imperfect flesh "is not under subjection to the law of God, nor, in fact, can it be," due to its sinful nature. (Rom. 8:7)

Consequently, Christians should constantly strive hard to weed out, yes, *root out,* these things from mind and heart, to harmonize their lives more fully with the truth, reflecting God's holiness to a greater degree. Each Christian should search his life-style and personality to endeavor to clear out all filthiness of flesh and spirit and all things detracting from his profession as a Christian— every vestige, as far as possible. The apostle Paul gave a fine reason for doing this. He said: "Therefore, since we have these promises, beloved ones, let us cleanse ourselves of every defilement of flesh and spirit, perfecting holiness in God's fear." (2 Cor. 7:1)

At 1 Peter 1:14-16, the apostle Peter expresses the thought: "As obedient children, quit being fashioned according to the desires you formerly had in your ignorance, but, in accord with the Holy One who called you, do you also become holy yourselves in all your conduct, because it is written: 'You must be holy, because I am holy.'" This does not mean that we should begin to consider ourselves holy on our own merit, hence, feeling superior to others. Since 'in our flesh dwells nothing good,' we have to keep up the fight to eliminate badness that constantly crops up. We must humbly recognize that we are undeserving sinners, hence, needing to 'perfect holiness.' (Isa. 65:5; Rom. 7:18; 1 John 1:8-10)

and accept with mildness the implanting of the word

The removal of badness from the heart and mind prepares the way for the "word" of truth to be implanted there and to flourish, like seed in a weed-free field. The Christian should not resist the "word" but should accept it in a spirit of mildness or gentleness, humbly yielding to its influence. (Acts 17:11, 12; compare 13:45, 46, 48.) This "implanting" does not merely apply to the initial planting of the "word" in a newly converted Christian. The meaning is that the Christian continually lets more truth be implanted in him from the truthful message of God now complete as written in the Bible. He accepts all that he hears with lowliness of heart and obedience, so that it sinks in and takes root in him. (Eph. 3:17-19; Col. 2:6, 7) Those who do this produce an abundance of fruit, as does the fine soil in the parable of the sower. (Matt. 13:23; Gal. 5:22, 23)

which is able to save your souls

With the aid of the holy spirit, the implanted "word" produces a new personality that conforms to the divine image. Hence, the Christian stands as approved before God and Christ. In this way the "word" plays a vital role in salvation. The apostle Paul tells us how the "word" should affect Christians: "Provided, indeed, that you heard [Christ] and were taught by means of him, just as truth is in Jesus, . . . you should put away the old personality which conforms to your former course of conduct and which is being corrupted according to [the personality's] deceptive desires; . . . you should be made new in the force actuating your mind, and should put on the new personality

22 However, become doers of the word, and not hearers only, deceiving yourselves with false reasoning.

---

which was created according to God's will in true righteousness and loyalty." (Eph. 4:21-24)

22 However, become doers of the word

As Christians, we need to apply the "word" of truth in our lives, show faith in its benefits, the wisdom inherent in it. We should constantly pay attention to that "word," letting it be our guide. Jesus pointed out: "Not everyone saying to me, 'Lord, Lord,' will enter into the kingdom of the heavens, but the one doing the will of my Father who is in the heavens will." (Matt. 7:21, 24-27) He also said: "Happy are those hearing the word of God and keeping it!" (Luke 11:28)

and not hearers only

Being a Christian is not a matter of merely listening respectfully to a discussion of the "word" of truth. Attendance at Christian meetings and reading the Scriptures are not enough. (The Greek word for "hearers" contains the idea of listeners to public reading of the Scriptures, as was done by Jewish worshipers. Some of them went to the synagogue diligently, hearing the Scriptures read again and again, but this did not produce faith that led to their recognition of the Messiah; likewise today with many listeners to Bible reading.) To be a genuine hearer is to have faith, and faith produces works. (Rom. 10:17; Jas. 2:20) A 'hearer only' would be one without faith.

deceiving yourselves with false reasoning

A person may think that, by attendance at Christian meetings, listening respectfully to what

23 For if anyone is a hearer of the word, and not a doer, this one is like a man looking at his natural face in a mirror.

---

is said and then engaging in personal reading of the Bible, he has fulfilled his religious duty. Yet, in other respects, his life may not be very different from that of persons who make no profession of being servants of God. In failing to recognize that true worship involves his *whole life,* the individual becomes guilty of self-deception. He loses sight of the fact that *obedience* to the "word" of truth is a divine requirement. Such deception can be a more formidable barrier to salvation and more difficult to overcome than ignorance or unbelief itself. (See also James 2:18, 19; 4:17.) Jehovah God exacts exclusive devotion, a devotion that reaches into every aspect of a person's life. (1 Cor. 10:31) The one who practices merely the outward forms of worship is failing in this respect.

23 For if anyone is a hearer of the word, and not a doer, this one is like a man looking at his natural face in a mirror

From his reflected image in the mirror, a

24 For he looks at himself, and off he goes and immediately forgets what sort of man he is.

---

man can see all his defects and blemishes. Presumably he looks so as to evaluate his appearance, consider it and correct, if possible, any irregularities his appearance manifests. What he looks like is conveyed to his mind. So, too, by hearing the "word" we can come to see ourselves for what we actually are.

24 For he looks at himself, and off he goes and immediately forgets what sort of man he is

A man before a mirror generally does not take long to form an opinion about his appearance. He may see signs of increasing age. Perhaps tension and sleepless nights have caused bags under his eyes. In some cases, dissipation leaves its marks. When before the mirror, he has a clear view of these things, which should give him concern and make him think seriously of how he has used his life and how he can improve the remaining years. But when he turns away, his interest in what his

25 But he who peers into the perfect law that belongs to freedom and who persists in it, this man, because he has become, not a forgetful hearer, but a doer of the work, will be happy in his doing it.

appearance was quickly fades. He may even prefer to forget some undesirable features. Away from the mirror and occupied with other things, he forgets all about his appearance, including what might be needed to correct it. (Compare 2 Peter 1:9.) It is different with the man who is a doer of the work. He peers into the perfect law.

25 But he who peers into the perfect law

The Greek expression for the verb "peers" denotes 'stooping beside something.' The idea is that of bending forward to look at an object very carefully. (Compare John 20:5, 11; 1 Peter 1:12.) The doer of the work does just that. He scrutinizes the perfect law with the desire to do it, seeing himself, his life, in relation thereto. That law, being perfect, is *complete,* embracing everything that is required of a Christian. It needs no addition of human traditions to fill it out or make up for any lack. Its commandments and principles are a perfect guide to right conduct that will lead on to salvation and God's approval. (Prov. 30:5, 6; Ps. 119:105, 140)

that belongs to freedom

This law goes along with the freedom enjoyed by God's people. Such freedom is opposite to enslavement to sin and death. The expression "law that belongs to freedom" points to the new covenant, the laws of which are written on hearts. (Jer. 31:33) Unlike the Mosaic law, which condemned the Israelites as sinners deserving of death, the "law that belongs to freedom" leads to life. (Rom. 7:5, 6, 9; 8:2, 4; 2 Cor. 3:6-9) Christians, therefore, are not under a lengthy code of rules and regulations, but are to be guided by God's revealed will. (Gal. 5:1, 13, 14) Hence, they act because of conscience toward God. What they do is from the heart, willingly, not under compulsion because of a code of rules with its penalties for violation. Since love is the very foundation of God's law, the Christian's worship is primarily positive, not negative. (Matt. 22:37-40; compare James 2:12.)

and who persists in it

To persist in the law that belongs to freedom means to do more than examine it. Such a man is different from the man who looks into a mirror and then forgets, losing interest in what the mirror revealed. The Christian 'remains beside' (*Kingdom Interlinear Translation*) the perfect law, that is, he "persists," continues to scrutinize it with the view of keeping his life in close conformity to it. (Ps. 119:9, 16, 97) There is a need to be absorbed fully with that law, letting it be our guide.

this man, because he has become, not a forgetful hearer, but a doer of the work, will be happy in his doing it

Because of applying the "word" in his daily life, the Christian demonstrates that he is not a forgetful hearer—not a person who may listen respectfully but who then fails to act on the information heard. He is really putting what he hears to work. As a result, he is happy. The perfect law brings him genuine benefits that make life far more enjoyable. (Ps. 19:7-11; compare 1 Timothy 4:8.) He enjoys the contentment and satisfaction that come from knowing that he is pleasing in Jehovah's sight.

26 If any man seems to himself to be a formal worshiper and yet does not bridle his tongue, but goes on deceiving his own heart, this man's form of worship is futile.

---

26 If any man seems to himself to be a formal worshiper

A man may imagine himself to be devout, fully dedicated to God. He may be doing even some righteous works, appearing in his own eyes to be a wholehearted worshiper. Yet there may be a grave flaw in his conduct—a flaw that would call into serious question his professing to be a Christian. The Christian's *entire* life course should harmonize with the "word" of truth. It must be from the heart, not a mere adherence to certain formalities or a prescribed routine. It is God's estimation of him, not his own, that really counts. (1 Cor. 4:4)

and yet does not bridle his tongue

The serious defect that James here mentions is a failure to keep the tongue in check from speaking what is bad. This would include slanderous talk, backbiting, rash statements, flattery, deceptive reasoning, and so forth. Whatever his pretensions, his speech condemns him as being hypocritical. The Pharisees were self-righteous, but with their tongues they flattered, lied, sought their own glory and spoke evil of those whom they considered inferior. (Mark 12:38-40; John 7:47, 48; compare Romans 3:10-18.)

but goes on deceiving his own heart

Self-righteousness brings self-deception. Christianity requires that our body members, including the tongue, be controlled. 'Every thought should be brought into captivity and made obedient to

27 The form of worship that is clean and undefiled from the standpoint of our God and Father
is this: to look after orphans and widows in their
tribulation, and to keep oneself without spot from
the world.

---

the Christ.' (2 Cor. 10:5) Therefore, the person
who thinks that he is living as a Christian and
yet leaves his tongue unbridled, to the hurt of
others, or to himself, is deceiving himself. He may
have many abilities, and even zeal and outward
benevolence. But he does not really appreciate
what it means to be a Christian. (1 Cor. 13:1-3)
No one who still carries on some God-dishonoring
practice can be a devoted servant of God. James
says more about the tongue in chapter 2.

this man's form of worship is futile

Since there is a major defect in the individual's
conduct, his worship is not acceptable to Jehovah.
It is not really worship of God, but a mere for-
malism, contaminated by his lack of control of
the tongue. Such supposed worship is defiled, unclean, and, therefore, futile or in vain. Compare
Haggai 2:14, where the prophet shows that Israel's
negligence in temple rebuilding made all their
works unclean from God's standpoint. They had
a form of worship, but it was of no value in
Jehovah's eyes.

**27 The form of worship that is clean and un-
defiled from the standpoint of our God and
Father is this**

The reference is to the worship that Jehovah
God views as "clean," pure, holy and "undefiled,"
untainted by any badness. Besides being the God
of Christians, Jehovah is also their Father, for
he has begotten them by means of his spirit to
be his sons. James is not trying to give a full

definition of true worship with all its requirements; he is not saying that caring for widows and orphans and keeping unspotted from the world are all that true worship amounts to. He is showing that genuine service to God is more than a form, carried on according to a set of rules, but one that reaches the heart and takes in the entire person and encompasses everything in his life, including sympathy and love for others. (1 John 3:18)

to look after orphans and widows in their tribulation

A distinguishing mark of true Christians is an active concern for the needy, including the orphans and widows who often find themselves among the afflicted, suffering tribulation. (Gal. 2:10) The Christian should be willing and eager to come to their aid. Properly motivated Christian giving is of great value in the sight of God. (2 Cor. 9:6-15; Heb. 6:10; 13:16) God reveals himself as the Protector of the fatherless boy and the widow. (Deut. 10:17, 18; Ps. 68:5)

From the very start, the early Christian congregation took special interest in providing for widows. (Acts 6:1-6) Jesus showed in the parable of the sheep and the goats that love and kind services rendered to the least of Christ's brothers in need provide a basis for favorable judgment. (Matt. 25:35, 36, 45) The apostle Paul admonishes: "Really, then, as long as we have time favorable for it, let us work what is good toward all, but especially toward those related to us in the faith." (Gal. 6:10; 1 John 3:14-18; Jas. 2: 14-17) Concern for the lowly and the needy also includes speaking consolingly with the comfort that the Scriptures give. This will provide spiritual upbuilding. (1 Thess. 5:14; 2 Cor. 1:3-5)

and to keep oneself without spot from the world

The "world" here, as in many places in the Bible, has reference to humans in general who are not serving God, but are "lying in the power of the wicked one." (1 John 5:19) The Christian should stand out as different from the world, as he should be no part of it. (John 17:14) We should remain free from the violence and corruption of the world, not partaking of its divisive politics, nationalism or unjust schemes. Also, we cannot be genuine Christians if we adopt any attitudes, speech or conduct that would be out of harmony with God's will. Even to take a course parallel to the world, doing the unrighteous things it does although without direct association with people of the world, would be just as corrupt in the eyes of God. We would still be spotted, tainted by the world. (Rom. 12:2) It must be kept in mind that such a thing is possible right in the congregation, as Paul warns Timothy: "Now in a large house there are vessels not only of gold and silver but also of wood and earthenware, and some for an honorable purpose but others for a purpose lacking honor. If, therefore, anyone keeps clear of the latter ones, he will be a vessel for an honorable purpose, sanctified, useful to his owner, prepared for every good work. So, flee from the desires incidental to youth, but pursue righteousness, faith, love, peace, along with those who call upon the Lord out of a clean heart." (2 Tim. 2:20-22)

QUESTIONS FOR STUDY

VERSE 1

James

1 What four men mentioned in the Greek Scriptures were named James?

2 How can we rule out, as writer of the letter of James: (a) the father of the faithful apostle Judas? (b) the apostle John's brother? (c) the apostle who was the son of Alphaeus?

3 What evidence can we give that points to James, Jesus' half brother, as the writer of the letter?

a slave of God and of the Lord Jesus Christ

1 Why does James speak of himself as a slave rather than as the brother of Jesus Christ?

2 How is the Christian a slave of both Christ and Jehovah?

to the twelve tribes

1 Who are the "twelve tribes" to whom James writes? Give reasons.

2 What makes a person a member of spiritual Israel?

that are scattered about

1 How did the spiritual "twelve tribes" come to be scattered?

Greetings!

1 According to the Greek, what is the literal meaning of the expression "Greetings!"?

2 How does the expression "Greetings!" partly support the evidence that the letter was written by James, the Lord's half brother?

VERSE 2

Consider it all joy

1 Why should Christians consider it "all joy" when trials occur?

my brothers

1 Why could James properly address the scattered Christians as "brothers"?

    2 What was James revealing about his attitude by addressing his readers as "my brothers"?

when you meet with various trials
    1 What things may trials include?
    2 Does the Christian "meet with" trials that are in addition to what the non-Christian encounters?

VERSE 3

knowing as you do that this tested quality of your faith works out endurance
    1 Why should trials, when they arise, be endured with "all joy" rather than with gloom?
    2 When our faith is proved by testing, what kind of endurance do we develop?

VERSE 4

But let endurance have its work complete
    1 Why is it best to face a trial without complaint and without giving in?

that you may be complete and sound in all respects, not lacking in anything
    1 What "work" does endurance perform in us?
    2 How will enduring faithfully make us "complete and sound in all respects"?

VERSE 5

So, if any one of you is lacking in wisdom
    1 What is wisdom?
    2 What particular wisdom is referred to here?
    3 If we do not have the needed wisdom, how may we react to a trialsome situation?

let him keep on asking God
    1 Why should we "keep on" asking God when we are under trial or facing difficult problems?

for he gives generously to all and without reproaching
    1 How does God give generously?
    2 In what way does God give without reproaching?

and it will be given him
    1 In what way will the wisdom God gives help us to meet a trial?
    2 What difference may there be in God's answering prayers of wisdom to face a trial from his answering other prayers?
    3 In what ways may we get the answer to our prayer for wisdom?

VERSE 6

But let him keep on asking in faith, not doubting at all

1 Describe the faith that we should have when asking God for wisdom.

for he who doubts is like a wave of the sea driven by the wind and blown about
1 In what condition is the person who doubts when he prays to God?

VERSE 7

In fact, let not that man suppose that he will receive anything from Jehovah
1 Why would God not grant a doubter the answer to his prayer?

VERSE 8

he is an indecisive man, unsteady in all his ways
1 How is the one who doubts in prayer like-minded in other matters of life?

VERSE 9

But let the lowly brother exult over his exaltation
1 In what way is the poor person who becomes a Christian exalted?
2 Is the poor person handicapped in any way as to his place in the congregation or in his service to God?

VERSE 10

and the rich one over his humiliation
1 How does becoming a Christian bring humiliation on the rich man?
2 Yet how can the rich man exult over this humiliation?

because like a flower of the vegetation he will pass away
1 Describe the passing away of the rich man "like a flower."

VERSE 11

For the sun rises with its burning heat and withers the vegetation, and its flower drops off and the beauty of its outward appearance perishes
1 How does James describe the action of the sun's heat on vegetation?

So, too, the rich man will fade away in his ways of life
1 How is the rich man compared to a flower, especially in its being withered by the sun's heat?
2 Yet how can a Christian who is rich get true enjoyment from his riches?

3 What contrast did King David make, showing that outward appearances are sometimes deceptive?

VERSE 12

Happy is the man that keeps on enduring trial

1 What does James mean here by the term "trial"?
2 Why does a man who endures a trial enjoy an increase in happiness?

because on becoming approved he will receive the crown of life

1 What is promised to the Christian who endures to the end through trials?
2 Does the faithfully enduring Christian earn life or receive it as wages or a reward? Explain.

which Jehovah promised to those who continue loving him

1 On what requirement is the receiving of the promise based?

VERSE 13

When under trial, let no one say: "I am being tried by God"

1 Into what wrong thinking may a Christian who is experiencing some adversity be led?
2 Is there any way that the Christian can be sure that he will be able to endure the trial successfully?

For with evil things God cannot be tried

1 Why is this statement true? (Compare Psalm 19: 7-10.)

nor does he himself try anyone

1 When we encounter a trialsome situation where we are tempted to sin, what view should we take?
2 Why can we view the trial as something that will work to our benefit?

VERSE 14

But each one is tried by being drawn out and enticed by his own desire

1 What causes a person under trial to sin?
2 If, in a certain circumstance, a person sins, whom should he rightly blame? Why?
3 What means are used, not by God, but by the world, to cause us to sin?
4 Why do we pray to God: "Do not bring us into temptation"?

5 Why was Jesus, by his trials and suffering, not enticed to do evil?

VERSE 15

Then the desire, when it has become fertile, gives birth to sin

1 Describe what brings a person to the point of sinning.
2 Does an individual have to commit an overt act in order to be sinning?

in turn, sin, when it has been accomplished, brings forth death

1 How may *any* sin lead a person into death?

VERSE 16

Do not be misled

1 How might a Christian under trial be misled?
2 Should we ever be in anxiety due to fear that we will not be able to endure a trial successfully?

my beloved brothers

1 What is shown here by James' addressing his readers as "brothers"?

VERSE 17

Every good gift and every perfect present is from above

1 What is often lacking in human gifts?
2 From where only do really perfect gifts come, and why can they be said to be perfect?

for it comes down from the Father of the celestial lights

1 Why can God be called "the Father of the celestial lights"?

and with him there is not a variation of the turning of the shadow

1 By what illustration can we explain the meaning of this statement?
2 How does this statement show that we can always put *complete* reliance on God?

VERSE 18

Because he willed it, he brought us forth by the word of truth

1 What is James speaking of as one of the very best of God's gifts?
2 By what means does God bring forth spiritual sons?

for us to be certain firstfruits of his creatures

1 How are the spirit-begotten sons of God a "certain firstfruits"?

2 What may James have had in mind with regard to the Israelite offerings on Nisan 16 and on Pentecost day?

VERSE 19

Know this, my beloved brothers

1 Why does James tell his readers, "Know this"?

2 How do John 13:17 and Jeremiah 22:16 demonstrate that what we really know should move us to act?

3 So, in effect, what is James saying?

Every man must be swift about hearing

1 What is the significance of the word "hearing," as used here?

2 What is involved in being "swift" about hearing?

slow about speaking

1 What would be included in the counsel to be "slow about speaking"?

2 What would be bad about being too quick to speak?

slow about wrath

1 How can we be wrong if anger causes us to speak too quickly?

2 Though in some cases we may be angry, what trouble will be avoided by 'slowing down' in our expression of anger?

VERSE 20

for man's wrath does not work out God's righteousness

1 Why will the righteousness that God requires of us never spring from a wrathful disposition?

2 Also, how does human wrath obscure God's righteousness?

VERSE 21

Hence put away all filthiness

1 Why must this be done?

and that superfluous thing, badness

1 Why is badness called the "superfluous thing"?

2 What effort should be put forth by the Christian, and how often, to get rid of this "superfluous thing"?

3 Does this mean that Christians finally get rid of *all* badness, so that they do not need to 'perfect holiness'?

and accept with mildness the implanting of the word

1 What must be done before the implanting of the word can take place?

2 How must the Christian accept the implanting of the word "with mildness"?

3 Does James refer to the implanting of the word only when one first becomes a Christian, or what?

which is able to save your souls

1 How is the implanted word able to save our souls?

2 How does the apostle Paul describe what is involved in growing to salvation?

VERSE 22

However, become doers of the word

1 How did Jesus view the importance of being doers of the word?

and not hearers only

1 Why are attending Christian meetings and reading the Scriptures not enough?

2 In relation to faith, what would a 'hearer only' be?

deceiving yourselves with false reasoning

1 Why is it so dangerous to be only a hearer of the word and not a doer?

2 Why, in some cases, may deception through false reasoning be a greater barrier than ignorance or unbelief?

VERSE 23

For if anyone is a hearer of the word, and not a doer, this one is like a man looking at his natural face in a mirror

1 When a man looks into a mirror, what is generally the purpose, and what does he see?

VERSE 24

For he looks at himself, and off he goes and immediately forgets what sort of man he is

1 How is a person who is a hearer and not a doer like the man who walks away from looking into a mirror?

VERSE 25

But he who peers into the perfect law

1 What is the meaning of the expression, 'he who peers into'?

2 What is "the perfect law"?

that belongs to freedom

1 What is the "law that belongs to freedom"?

2 How is the Christian's worship positive, not negative?

and who persists in it

1 What is the difference between the one who is like the person who looks into a mirror and the one who peers into the perfect law and "persists" in it?

this man, because he has become, not a forgetful hearer, but a doer of the work, will be happy in his doing it
1 How does a Christian demonstrate that he is not a forgetful hearer, and what is the result to him?

VERSE 26

If any man seems to himself to be a formal worshiper
1 Why is seeming, even to one's own self, to be a formal worshiper not enough?

and yet does not bridle his tongue
1 What kind of talk can result from failure to bridle the tongue?

but goes on deceiving his own heart
1 In what way is the Christian who does not bridle his tongue "deceiving his own heart"?

this man's form of worship is futile
1 Why is one who lets his tongue go unbridled practicing a futile form of worship?
2 How does Haggai 2:14 illustrate that this is the case?

VERSE 27

The form of worship that is clean and undefiled from the standpoint of our God and Father is this
1 How is God also the Father to Christians?
2 Is James here describing all that there is to true Christianity?

to look after orphans and widows in their tribulation
1 What is an essential and distinguishing mark of all true Christians, as shown here by James?
2 How do we know that God sets great value on Christian giving and the rendering of help to those who are in need, or afflicted?
3 Show the importance placed on helping needy, lonesome or oppressed ones in the early Christian congregation.

and to keep oneself without spot from the world
1 What is "the world" here referred to?
2 What does the expression 'to be no part of the world' mean and include?
3 Is it possible, or likely, that any persons in the Christian congregation may not be unspotted from the world?

CHAPTER 2

1 My brothers, you are not holding the faith of our Lord Jesus Christ, our glory, with acts of favoritism, are you?

---

1 My brothers

Though James was giving strong reproof regarding some very unchristian attitudes, he addressed his readers as *brothers,* showing that he did not feel that they had fallen away from the truth; they were a part of God's congregation. But James continues to point out the vanity of a professed religion that may be quite vocal but does not manifest itself in right conduct and true, impartial love.

The Wickedness of Favoritism

you are not holding the faith

Faith in Jesus Christ is the basic essential of Christianity. But the readers of James' letter were not holding firmly to the teachings and spirit of Christ, their partiality violating the principles of unity and love.

of our Lord Jesus Christ, our glory

The Greek expression translated "our glory" is understood to be in apposition with or equivalent to Jesus Christ. He is the One in whom the Christian brothers should boast. He was "received up in glory." (1 Tim. 3:16) As to the future, he is the one who comes "with power and great glory," who sits on "his glorious throne." (Matt. 24:30; 25:31)

This reference to faith in their glorious Lord would serve to emphasize James' counsel that the

2 For, if a man with gold rings on his fingers and
in splendid clothing enters into a gathering of you,
but a poor man in filthy clothing also enters,

---

brothers should not be assigning special glory or
honor to rich or well-dressed men who attended
meetings, thus discriminating against the poor
ones attending. This would detract from their
appreciation of Jesus Christ. Not material riches,
but faith in this glorious Lord was what really
mattered.

with acts of favoritism, are you?

To favor one person over another, and especially
because one is rich, prominent or powerful, and
the other poor and lowly, would be the very opposite of Christianity. It would be downgrading
Jesus Christ who, when on earth, was materially
poor, as were most of his disciples. (2 Cor. 8:9;
6:10) Yet Jesus himself was the one in whom
they should boast. Compare the statement of the
Law, at Leviticus 19:15, commanding that no one
should be favored, either because he is rich or
because he is poor.

2 For, if a man with gold rings on his fingers and in splendid clothing enters into a gathering of you

Visitors, *unbelievers*, might walk into the place
where the Christians held their meeting, as Paul
mentions at 1 Corinthians 14:23, 24. The man
whom James describes was wealthy, richly and
smartly dressed, possibly ostentatious; he was
doubtless a prominent man in the community.

but a poor man in filthy clothing also enters

The poor man is also a *visitor*. If he wanted to
become a baptized member of the congregation

3 yet you look with favor upon the one wearing the splendid clothing and say: "You take this seat here in a fine place," and you say to the poor one: "You keep standing," or: "Take that seat there under my footstool,"

---

despite attending the meetings dressed in vile or filthy, shabby clothing, the members of the congregation would help him to see the need to dress in a clean, neat way and, if necessary, they would give him assistance in getting something more presentable to wear. (Compare 1 Timothy 2:9, 10; Romans 12:13.) As long as he is an unbeliever, he should be welcomed as cordially as the rich man, to hear the "good news" discussed. Of course, the *principle* of impartiality would apply to believers as well as unbelievers.

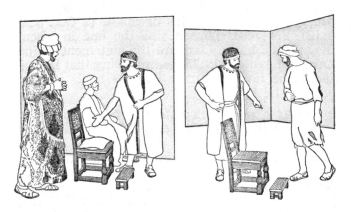

3 yet you look with favor upon the one wearing the splendid clothing and say: "You take this seat here in a fine place"

Or, 'please sit over here,' perhaps in one of the most prominent or desirable seats. James condemned, not the courtesy itself, but the fact that special attention or deference was accorded the person merely because he seemed to be a person of rank, or a rich man.

and you say to the poor one: "You keep standing," or: "Take that seat there under my footstool"

He gets coolly welcomed, and is then told: 'Stand over there, or sit on the floor by my footstool.' (Sitting on the floor with legs crossed was a common Eastern posture; more prominent persons often had chairs, benches, and so forth.) The poor man was counted unworthy of any special attention, such as was granted to the rich man. Some believe that a responsible person in the congregation, an elder or a "deacon," is represented as speaking to the rich man and to the poor man, particularly since reference is made to a "footstool." Of course, we have today no direct testimony as to what Christian meeting places in the first century were like. However, the fact that James begins this portion with the expression "my brothers," and uses the plural form throughout in addressing them, may weigh in favor of James' example being one that applied to all members of the congregation generally.*

But the congregation was acting like the Pharisees, who looked upon the common people

---

* The commentary by Bible scholar F. C. Cook says: "Some suppose that a bustling official is represented, marshalling the congregation to seats according to rank. But this is an anachronism [that is, something placed out of its proper time]. It is the *officious* act of one who himself has a good seat ('*here* in a good place') with a 'footstool;' and who offers the rich man a similar one." *The Interpreter's Bible* commentary says: "The speaker in vs. 3 does not appear to be an official appointed to attend to visitors, but is a member of the congregation sitting in a comfortable seat provided with a footstool. He rises and offers the wealthy stranger this seat but contemptuously gives the poor man only the choice between standing or sitting on the floor."

4 you have class distinctions among yourselves and you have become judges rendering wicked decisions, is that not so?

---

as 'people of the earth.' With regard to those who listened to Jesus, the Pharisees argued: "Not one of the rulers or of the Pharisees has put faith in him, has he? But this crowd that does not know the Law are accursed people." (John 7:48, 49)

4 you have class distinctions among yourselves

By this action the congregation was making divisions in the body of Christ, his congregation, in contradiction of the principle expressed by the apostle Paul: "There is neither Jew nor Greek, there is neither slave nor freeman, there is neither male nor female; for you are all one person in union with Christ Jesus." (Gal. 3:28) Whether the difference be with regard to wealth, education, profession, social status, race or language, there is no basis for partiality. In the face of the temptation to cater to the rich and prominent, members of the congregation failed to show decisiveness, wavered (as noted in James 1:6), and were not acting out of real faith. They departed from the faith of "our Lord Jesus Christ, our glory," the one who, though rich, emptied himself and 'became poor that we might become rich through his poverty.' (Phil. 2:7; 2 Cor. 8:9) Their faith in Jesus Christ should have taught them better. (Eph. 4:20, 21) Something was wrong with their faith, to count the life of one man as of more value than that of another in the eyes of God, and of Christ, who died for that person. (1 Sam. 16:7; 2 Cor. 5:14; Rom. 5:6) They showed a divided allegiance, even as does one who divides his devotion between God and Mammon, or riches. (Matt. 6:24)

5 Listen, my beloved brothers. God chose the
ones who are poor respecting the world to be rich
in faith and heirs of the kingdom, which he promised to those who love him, did he not?

---

and you have become judges rendering wicked
decisions, is that not so?

They presumed to become judges of men, assessing their individual, personal worth, and even
their comparative worth from God's standpoint.
Furthermore, they did it, not on moral grounds,
but with the improper motive of honoring men
on account of their appearance or position. They
thus compounded the wrong, for they judged by
false standards. Their decisions implied that a
rich man was more deserving of hearing the
"good news" than a poor man. This was out of
harmony with the fact that God himself and
Christ are impartial. (Acts 10:34) Such decisions
were not merely wrong but literally "wicked"
(the Greek term for which often implies being
harmful, hateful, unkind, cruel; compare 2 Thessalonians 3:2; Acts 17:5; Matthew 5:39; 18:32;
20:15; 1 Timothy 6:4). They were disrespecting
Christ Jesus, their glorious Lord, who certainly
made no distinctions in favor of outward appearance, and they tarnished the glory that Christ
bestowed on them as his congregation.

5 Listen, my beloved brothers

James' counsel was given out of love. He recognized that the brothers were exhibiting many
good traits and showed love for Christ and their
fellow Christians; nevertheless, they were imperfect and had fallen into a bad way. He trusted
and hoped that, with correction, they would recover.

God chose the ones who are poor respecting the world

God, of course, accepts the rich as readily as the poor, not favoring either above the other. But circumstances make it more likely that the one poor in this world's goods will listen with greater readiness to the "good news." Material wealth is so often an obstacle to faith in God. (Matt. 19:23, 24) Sometimes those who get wealth have done so selfishly, at the expense of others. Many achieve riches or prominence by catering to those in power and by maneuvering to gain position, often by talking against others whom they consider rivals. Therefore, because of their selfish hearts, God does not choose such ones. They, and some others who attain their riches honestly and honorably, are 'having their consolation in full' now. (Luke 6:24) While neither great riches nor poverty is desirable, the poor or "common" people are generally more responsive to the comfort that the "good news" brings. (Prov. 30:8, 9; 1 Cor. 1:26-29) God draws such ones to Christ. (John 6:44, 45; Acts 16:14; 13:48) So, what James said was in no way a commendation or glorification of poverty in itself, but a recognition of what was factual, in accord with reality.

Again, those who are poor may have had their eyes opened to the injustices of this world and the futility of the present system of things. (Compare Ezekiel 9:4.) They see the need of something better, and are generally more likely to become "conscious of their spiritual need." (Matt. 5:3, 4) Of course, the ones chosen are not all poor persons. James, in effect, points out to the brothers that the poor visitor is more likely to become a believer than the rich one, yet they, paradoxically, are showing partiality to the rich and prominent.

to be rich in faith and heirs of the kingdom

They, regardless of material possessions, are rich because of having faith. God chooses them to be rich *through* their faith. Faith of itself is a real treasure and is not the possession of many. (2 Thess. 3:2) It also leads to other riches. The apostle Paul, who suffered much in order to be able to serve others, spoke of himself and his co-workers as "poor but making many rich, as having nothing and yet possessing all things." (2 Cor. 6:10; compare 1 Corinthians 4:8-13; Revelation 2:9.) By the exercise of faith, the persons to whom these bore witness would gain such spiritual riches. They are not like the wealthy man who reveled in his possessions but was not rich toward God, lacking faith. (Luke 12:16-21) Those not having faith are actually poor in God's eyes. (Compare Revelation 3:17, 18.) What riches does faith bring to those whom God 'chooses'? Besides benefiting from the riches of God's mercy, his kindness, forbearance and long-suffering, and enjoying the wisdom that the "word of the Christ" brings to those exercising faith, they have the grand prospect of being heirs with God's Son. (Compare Romans 2:4; Ephesians 1:7, 18; Colossians 3:16.)

Those thus "rich in faith" are therefore heirs of the Kingdom. Those spirit-begotten ones exercising such faith are now 'transferred into the kingdom of the Son of his love,' and have the hope of eventually sharing with Christ in his heavenly rule through a resurrection of the dead. (Col. 1:13; 1 Pet. 1:3, 4) To his disciples who had faith, Jesus said: "Happy are you poor, because yours is the kingdom." (Luke 6:20)

which he promised to those who love him, did he not?

It is not that they initially love God so much, but that on learning of God's love for mankind

6 You, though, have dishonored the poor man. The rich oppress you, and they drag you before law courts, do they not?

---

they respond with love for God. (1 John 4:10) They come to know more about God, becoming intimates of his, and they develop more and more love for God as a fruit of the spirit. (Gal. 5:22) It is for these that the kingdom of God is an inheritance.

6 You, though, have dishonored the poor man

By showing favoritism to the rich, they were treating the poor without due respect, shabbily, and were insulting the ones whom God is pleased

to exalt. (Jas. 1: 9) How many of the congregation were from among the wealthy class? Likely only a few. (1 Cor. 1: 26-29) Where, then, would most of that very congregation be if God had treated them with contempt because they were poor or "ordinary" people? (Compare 1 Corinthians 11: 22.)

The rich oppress you, and they drag you before law courts, do they not?

Aside from persecuting the poor because of religion, the rich were often their oppressors in

7 They blaspheme the fine name by which you were called, do they not?

---

connection with wages, debts, rents, and in legal action over these matters. (Compare James 5:4.) Also, the rich often led the persecutors. The wealthy Sadducees were the ones who "laid their hands" on Peter and John, and, later, on the apostles. (Acts 4:1-3; 5:17, 18) The "reputable women" and the "principal men of the city" of Antioch in Pisidia were the ones whom the Jews stirred up against Paul and Barnabas. (Acts 13:50) At Philippi, the wealthy owners of a demon-possessed girl caused Paul and Silas to be thrown into jail. (Acts 16:16, 19, 23, 24) The craftsmen who made silver shrines of Artemis caused a great uproar at Ephesus against the teaching of the "good news" because they feared that they would lose profits. (Acts 19:23-28)

Certainly not all the rich people acted in this way, but James speaks of what the facts reveal to be the general rule. Obviously, not all the poor people were good, either. They were the ones usually stirred up by their leaders. (Compare Acts 17:5.) Some were poor because of sheer laziness or lack of self-discipline. (Prov. 6:9-11; 20:13; 23:21) But Christians were acting foolishly to give preference by catering to the very ones who generally, as a class, were opposers and oppressors.

7 They blaspheme the fine name by which you were called, do they not?

Blasphemy is injurious speech, especially applying to irreverent allusion to God and sacred things. In persecuting Christians, the opposers blasphemed the name by which these were called, the name of Christ, and even those not committing

8 If, now, you practice carrying out the kingly law according to the scripture: "You must love your neighbor as yourself," you are doing quite well.

---

open persecution spoke evil of Christ and of those bearing his name, thereby also blaspheming God, who sent Christ. (Compare John 13:20.)

8 If, now, you practice carrying out the kingly law according to the scripture: "You must love your neighbor as yourself," you are doing quite well

This law is called the "kingly law" or "royal law" because it rightly has the prominence and importance among other laws governing human relationships that a king would have among men.* Along with the law to love God, 'the whole Law and the Prophets hang upon' this law to 'love one's neighbor as oneself.' (Matt. 22:37-40) And the apostle Paul says: "The entire Law stands fulfilled" in such love. (Gal. 5:14; Rom. 13:10; compare 1 John 4:20.) This kingly law had been stated in the earlier Law code at Leviticus 19:18.

James says to those addressed in his letter that, 'if you practice carrying out that kingly law, you are doing quite well.' This calls to mind James' similar expression (in verse 19) with regard to some proclaiming their belief in one God. Throughout his letter James shows an awareness of the thinking of his brothers and frequently presents the viewpoint that his readers have, or might have, on the subject under discussion, and this insight gives unusual force to his letter. (Compare James 1:13, 26; 2:14; 3:13; 4:13.) We do not know whether James had heard some brothers

---

* *The Jerusalem Bible* renders this phrase as "the supreme law."

justify their very hospitable treatment of the rich
on the claim that this was simply showing 'love
of neighbor.' If any did, James' letter would bring
home to them how erroneous it would be to think
that showing love to some (such as the rich
man) could justify their failure to show the same
love to others (such as the poor man). To any
making such profession, the point would be,
'Showing neighbor love is fine, but is it to be
shown only to a certain class? What of the others?
Do you accord them all the same treatment?' So,
obedience to one precept (such as that found at
Leviticus 19:18) would never justify disobedience
to another (such as that found at Leviticus 19:15),
and this is a point James emphasizes subsequently
in verses 10, 11.

Likewise, if any felt that James' previous strong
statements regarding the rich class constituted
some contradiction of the law to love one's neighbor, then James' remarks here would refute such
an idea. The rich were included in the command
to love one's neighbor, and to treat them with
love was good. But so were the poor included,
and to exclude them was not full obedience to the
kingly law of love. Jesus, in discussing this same
kingly law, showed that many persons only carried it out to a certain extent, partially, not in
its full scope. He showed that, if they would be
perfect, complete, like their heavenly Father, they
needed to be impartial in their practicing of that
law of love. (Matt. 5:43-48) So, *to the extent* that
the congregation was carrying out that royal law,
they could be commended as "doing quite well."
It was good to show love and kindness to anyone
at any time. However, the same courtesy and love
extended to the rich should be shown to the poor.
Both should be treated equally as neighbors; no
one should be mistreated.

9 But if you continue showing favoritism, you are working a sin, for you are reproved by the law as transgressors.

10 For whoever observes all the Law but makes a false step in one point, he has become an offender against them all.

---

9 But if you continue showing favoritism, you are working a sin

These brothers needed to go further in order truly to follow the written Law code, for it forbade injustice and partiality to rich or to poor. (Lev. 19:15) So, if a Christian shows kindness and attention to a rich man, he 'does well,' provided that he also shows the same kindness to the poor man. If he is partial, he is sinning. According to the kingly law, he should love all his neighbors. If he violates that law by showing favoritism, he is a sinner. He 'misses the mark' (which is the meaning of the Greek term for sin) as to being like his heavenly Father in this regard.

for you are reproved by the law as transgressors

Since God himself requires impartiality in showing love, the one showing favoritism to one person above another while claiming to live by the royal law is thoroughly exposed as being in the wrong. He is a transgressor of the kingly law. Christians today must demonstrate their real Christianity, avoiding all partiality and class distinctions, in the face of all the world's class distinctions resulting from its social, cultural, racial and religious differences.

10 For whoever observes all the Law but makes a false step in one point

No one could actually observe all the commandments of the Law without a mistake, nor could any man even keep all but one of the Law's 600 or so points. (Jas. 3:2) But James is reproving the individual who claims to keep practically all the Law, and therefore, to be righteous. It is the tendency of men to choose the parts of the Scriptures that they want to follow, but to minimize the importance of the other parts.

he has become an offender against them all

The Law made up of many decrees is an entirety and is not to be fractionalized. (Col. 2:13, 14, 16; Gal. 5:14) Consequently, if a person breaks one of the commandments of the Law, he mars the whole code, and thus he is "an offender against them all." A person cannot claim that he is really being obedient to God and showing love to him and at the same time be violating any part of his law. In worldly courts, a person is tried for breaking a specific law. Say, for example, that a man embezzles a sum of money. It may be true that he has always kept *all* the other laws; this violation is his first offense. Yet his past record does not excuse him before the court for breaking this law regarding embezzling. He is treated as a transgressor of the law for that offense, a lawbreaker, no matter how upright he may be in other matters (though his sentence may be lighter than that of a habitual lawbreaker). The judge does not say, 'He kept a thousand other laws; he only broke the one on stealing, so we will excuse him for breaking this one.'

According to the foregoing facts, the Mosaic law showed all to be sinners because no one could keep it perfectly. The apostle Paul explained: "Now the Law does not adhere to faith, but 'he that does them shall live by means of them [by actual obedience to every commandment].' " (Gal. 3:12) It is not through the *attempted* keeping of that law that one can be justified before God—he is, instead, actually *convicted* as a transgressor because of not *really keeping* the law. "Cursed is

11 For he who said: "You must not commit adultery," said also: "You must not murder." If, now, you do not commit adultery but you do murder, you have become a transgressor of law.

---

every one that does not continue in all the things written in the scroll of the Law in order to do them," say the Scriptures. (Gal. 3:10) Only through faith in Christ's atoning sacrifice can forgiveness of sin and real relief come. Christ was the *one* man who kept the Law in all its parts, perfectly. He fulfilled the whole Law and therefore was used in the abolition of it. (Eph. 2:15) No man can be exempt from condemnation except by exercising faith in him. Paul writes: "Now we know that all the things the Law says it addresses to those under the Law, so that every mouth may be stopped and all the world may become liable to God for punishment. Therefore by works of law no flesh will be declared righteous before him, for by law is the accurate knowledge of sin." (Rom. 3:19, 20)

11 For he who said: "You must not commit adultery," said also: "You must not murder"

The law commanding a man to love his neighbor is an integral part of the Mosaic law along with the Ten Commandments. This is true of all the other commandments. However, James evidently chooses to cite these two commands as examples for the reason that he intends to show, later, that friendship with the world constitutes "adultery," and a hateful, loveless attitude toward one's brother would be "murder." (Jas. 4:2, 4)

If, now, you do not commit adultery but you do murder, you have become a transgressor of law

The *one* God, who deals with all in an unwaver-

12 Keep on speaking in such a way and keep on doing in such a way as those do who are going to be judged by the law of a free people.

---

ing, undivided and impartial way, was the Giver of the whole Law, including the law about love of neighbor. (Deut. 6:4) The Law was a unit. Consequently, to break one point in the Law was to offend the one and the same Giver of all the laws. The breaking of one part of God's law was therefore an offense against the entire Law, the whole code of law.

12 Keep on speaking in such a way and keep on doing in such a way as those do who are going to be judged by the law of a free people

The Mosaic law code was not "the law of a free people," or, literally, a law of freedom. (Gal. 4:24-26) This freedom is embodied in a people, the spiritual Israel. If judged by the Mosaic law they would be condemned as lawbreakers, hence, not innocent persons. Accordingly, they should speak and act with full recognition of the fact that they will not be judged by Mosaic law, but by another law, "the law of a free people," or, literally, a "law of freedom" (*Kingdom Interlinear Translation*)—as a people not enslaved to sin, which sin the Mosaic law in reality accentuated. (Rom. 7:8, 10) The "twelve tribes" of spiritual Israel are not under the Mosaic law. They are under the "law" of the new covenant. (Jer. 31: 31-33) Their words and works will be judged by God, under the provisions of his new covenant. (1 Pet. 2:16)

This "law of a free people" does not free spiritual Israelites from obedience to God, for he writes his law in their hearts. Through a living faith in Christ, they are confident that they will receive judgment as he has promised. Jehovah

13 For the one that does not practice mercy will
have his judgment without mercy. Mercy exults
triumphantly over judgment.

God will count their good works as evidence of
their faith. Jesus Christ, his Son, is the mediator
of the new covenant, and it is on the basis of his
propitiatory sacrifice that the new covenant is
established and that God may carry out the words
of that covenant, namely: "I shall forgive their
error, and their sin I shall remember no more."
(Jer. 31:34) Accordingly, spiritual Israelites under
the "law of freedom" conduct themselves, not as
though God is one who is looking for a fault in
them, but as those who keep "walking" with him,
jealously guarding their covenant relationship
with him. (Ps. 130:3, 4; Mic. 6:8)

**13 For the one that does not practice mercy will
have his judgment without mercy**

James points to a judgment, and he shows the
danger into which those showing favoritism were
putting themselves. (Rom. 2:6, 16; 14:12; Matt.
12:36) How could they expect mercy from God
when they withheld mercy from a man merely
because he was "a poor man in filthy clothing"?
(Jas. 2:2) How inconsistent and contrary to all
reason, that those to whom James wrote included
lowly persons, yet they discriminated against the
poor man! How would "poor" members feel if they
visited another congregation of Christians and
were insulted in this way? Proverbs 21:13 reads:
"As for anyone stopping up his ear from the
complaining cry of the lowly one, he himself also
will call and not be answered." Jesus said: "With
what judgment you are judging, you will be
judged." (Matt. 7:1, 2) He gave a powerful illustration of this point at Matthew 18:23-35.

14 Of what benefit is it, my brothers, if a certain one says he has faith but he does not have works? That faith cannot save him, can it?

Mercy exults triumphantly over judgment

"Happy are the merciful, since they will be shown mercy," Jesus said. (Matt. 5:7) In a legal court, a man who had exercised mercy toward others would not likely be excused from the penalty for the crime of which he was found guilty, though the punishment might possibly be mitigated somewhat. However, James is not speaking about transgressions under the Mosaic law or under a worldly law. He is here talking about judgment by the "law of freedom." A man in whose mind and heart mercy has been produced by God's spirit, as a result of his faith in Christ, is moved to show mercy in all his dealings. In consequence, he will receive mercy when he comes before judgment. Therefore this merciful person need not be fearful of judgment but can have confidence that he will experience mercy. He will not be condemned. Thus, he triumphs or gains a victory over strict justice or adverse judgment. A notable illustration of merciful concern for others and its effect on judgment is found in the parable of the sheep and the goats, at Matthew 25:32-40. Also, we may consider the mercy that Jehovah exercised toward David, who had in the past shown himself merciful. (2 Sam. 12:13, 14; 22:24-27; Ps. 18:23-26)

14 Of what benefit is it, my brothers, if a certain one says he has faith but he does not have works?

It should be noted that James is not contradicting what Paul says, namely, that "a man is declared righteous by faith apart from works of law." (Rom. 3:28) James fully agrees with this teaching, but he writes to refute an abuse or perversion of it. The perversion was the view that a man, by merely holding correct ideas about being justified by faith, without demonstrating that faith at all by doing good works, would be righteous in God's sight and would eventually receive complete salvation. Actually, James pointed out, any so-called faith that does not prompt the person to do good works is not genuine faith. Such a man only *"says* he has faith." The man who claims to have faith in Christ's atonement sacrifice, and says that he is a Christian, but who does not demonstrate that faith by action, is not in reality a Christian. If his "faith" did not make any changes in his personality, his life, his actions, what good would it be? How could he do as Jesus commanded his followers: "Let your light shine before men, that they may see your fine works and give glory to your Father who is in the heavens"? (Matt. 5:16)

True Faith Will Produce Fine Works

Would anyone call a man a real doctor, a dedicated physician, who set himself up in office as a doctor and expressed faith in medical treatment, yet never treated or helped another person medically? Jesus said: "Not everyone saying to me, 'Lord, Lord,' will enter into the kingdom of the heavens, but the one doing the will of my Father who is in the heavens will." (Matt. 7:21) What James says in verse 14 ties in with his description at chapter 1:26, 27, where he speaks of the man who "seems to himself" or 'thinks himself' to be a worshiper of God but fails in producing any fruitage of his faith or his form of worship. He fails to "bridle his tongue," discipline it to speak in accord with what is the true state of matters, what he actually is. His form of worship is "futile." He also fails to have works, such as looking after orphans and widows and keeping himself unspotted from the world. Furthermore, such hollow, futile profession of faith leads a person into such wrongs as the showing of partiality, into failing to fulfill the law of love and neglecting to show mercy. (Jas. 2:8, 9, 13)

That faith cannot save him, can it?

Note that James emphasizes, not faith itself, but the particular "faith" in question, *"that* faith," a falsely called faith that is without works. As James recognizes, true faith in God's word can save our souls. (Jas. 1:21) In this, James agrees fully with Paul. They are both in harmony as regards true faith and Christian works. But James is discussing works different from those that Paul writes about in Romans chapters 3 and 4.

Paul, in saying that works cannot bring one a declaration of righteousness, is talking about works of law that a person engaged in, works on which he might rely, thinking that he could *earn* righteousness from God, or, thinking that a Christian's continued good works *of themselves* would be what would gain righteousness for him. (Rom. 4:2-5) But James speaks about Christian works that are *motivated,* not by a law code, but by faith and love. They are a result, a product and a fruitage of that faith and cannot be separated or divorced from true faith. However, Paul, while pointing out that a person is initially declared righteous through faith, also spoke repeatedly of the need for the Christian to do works of faith—works manifesting that faith. He calls Christians a people "zealous for fine works." (Titus 2:14; compare 1 Thessalonians 1:2-7; 1 Timothy 2:10; Titus 2:7; 3:8, 14.) And who performed more works than Paul did? James asks: "That faith [that is, one not having works to show its genuineness] cannot save him, can it?" Clearly, the answer is: No, it cannot.

15 If a brother or a sister is in a naked state and lacking the food sufficient for the day, **16** yet a certain one of you says to them: "Go in peace, keep warm and well fed," but you do not give them the necessities for their body, of what benefit is it?

---

15 If a brother or a sister is in a naked state and lacking the food sufficient for the day, 16 yet a certain one of you says to them: "Go in peace, keep warm and well fed," but you do not give them the necessities for their body, of what benefit is it?

By "naked" James means not necessarily nude but insufficiently clad (the Greek word *gymnos* can be used in this sense). James here presents a forceful example. Kind words, thoughts or wishes given by a person, but not accompanied by tangible aid though he is able to help materially, are of no aid but are actually a mockery and may aggravate the pain of the suffering one. (Compare Proverbs 3: 27, 28.) Likewise, a so-called faith that does nothing and exerts no practical influence on the life of

17 Thus, too, faith, if it does not have works, is dead in itself.

18 Nevertheless, a certain one will say: "You have faith, and I have works. Show me your faith apart from the works, and I shall show you my faith by my works."

---

the individual, nor moves others to faith, is useless. One who would say, "Go in peace," while turning away the sufferer in his destitute state, leaving the job of helping him to someone else, would be known in the community as having no love or kindness. Likewise, the professing Christian with such an empty faith would reveal the worthlessness of his religion, bringing reproach on God. Could this be called Christianity? Would he be following the example of Christ? The patriarch Job, in a similar illustration, shows the adverse judgment that he himself would have received if he had followed this pattern. (Job 31:16-22)

17 Thus, too, faith, if it does not have works, is dead in itself

The kind of faith that does not have any action in harmony with its profession not only does nothing for the possessor thereof; it also has no influence with men, and none with God, any more than a dead person can exert influence with the living. (Compare Ecclesiastes 9:5, 6.) It is dead "according to itself." (*Kingdom Interlinear Translation*) That is, according to what evidence it presents, such "faith" provides *no proof* of having any life, despite the claims of the person possessing it that it does.

18 Nevertheless, a certain one will say: "You have faith, and I have works. Show me your faith apart from the works, and I shall show you my faith by my works."

In this case, James is using a literary device. Evidently anticipating that there would be persons associated with the Christian congregation who would raise objections to his inspired statements about faith and works, he has "a certain one" direct the foregoing quoted words to another member of the congregation.

If regarded as *a person who supports the argument* of James, the "certain one" is speaking to an objector who believes that mere faith is enough. To the objector, that one says: "You [claim to] have faith, and I have works." Continuing, the "certain one" presents the challenge: "Show me your [supposed] faith apart from the works, and I [who support the argument of James] shall show you my faith by my works." Really, the person claiming to have faith but having no works to prove its existence would not actually have real faith that leads to salvation. His supposed faith would be a lifeless sham.

On the other hand, James may have intended to cast the "certain one" in the role of *an objector* to the discussion of faith and works. The fact that James starts out with the Greek word meaning "but" or "nevertheless" lends support to this conclusion. The objector's statement to another member of the congregation would then be: "You have faith, and I have works." Or, as *The New English Bible* renders these words, "But someone may object: 'Here is one who claims to have faith and another who points to his deeds.' " (Since the quotation marks do not appear in the original Greek, the 'certain one's' statement may be viewed as ending here.*)

How might we understand the words that James placed in the mouth of such an individual? The

---

* Other translations that place only the first sentence ("You have faith, and I have works") in quotations include the *Revised Standard Version; The Twentieth Century New Testament,* the *New International Version; An American Translation; The New Berkeley Version* and *Today's English Version.*

person being portrayed would be one who believes that James is wrong in his argument. The individual is assuring or comforting another member of the congregation, a member who has a claimed faith without works. He says, in effect, to the one without works: 'Your faith is sufficient. One member of the congregation may have faith and another, works. This is all right. Faith and works are like different gifts—no one person can have all the many endowments found among the members of the Christian congregation. Do not be disturbed. James is making too much of works. Go ahead and rest assured that, even if you do not have works (such as the providing of food and clothing for needy brothers and sisters as James referred to in verses 15 and 16), you are fully pleasing to God if you have faith.'

James then answers:* "Show me your faith apart from the works, and I shall show you my faith by my works." In other words, he challenges the one professing to have faith without works to substantiate his claim, which has no tangible works to back it up. James, on the other hand, has deeds to prove the existence of genuine faith.

Whichever view is taken with regard to the placement of the quotation marks, it is clear that the basic point being made is the same, namely, the true Christian must have both faith and works.

The faith here professed is the basic faith in Jesus Christ and is essential for a Christian. The mere profession of it, however, does not prove its existence. Real faith has works *bound up with it*. Faith without works is not true faith, and anyone trying to identify and see such faith cannot find any trace of it, for it produces no evi-

---

* There is a possibility that James, in order to avoid emphasizing his own righteous deeds may be portraying a third person, one whom he presents as supporting his view and countering with the words: "Show me your faith apart from the works, and I shall show you my faith by my works."

19 You believe there is one God, do you? You are doing quite well. And yet the demons believe and shudder.

---

dence of its existence. Those areas in which good works should be in evidence turn out to be empty. Real faith and works cannot be separated. So the rebuttal set forth by James shows that there is substance to genuine faith. Such faith demonstrates its power to move the Christian to produce works.

What do these works include? In all areas of life, the Christian should want to conform to the divine will, 'doing all things for God's glory.' (1 Cor. 10:31) As shown in Jesus' illustration of the sheep and the goats, works of faith would include coming to the aid of Christ's spiritual brothers, comforting them in times of illness and supplying the needy among them with food, drink, clothing and shelter. (Matt. 25:35, 36) Vital, too, is the fine work of declaring the "good news." (Matt. 24:14) The faith that lacks such works is proved to be powerless, ineffective, nothing more than a mere claim.

19 You believe there is one God, do you? You are doing quite well

James selects the most obvious, basic truth of all worship, namely, that there is only one God, the Almighty. Clearly, this one God in whom James' readers believed was the God who identifies himself in the inspired Scriptures. In having this faith a Christian would be doing well as far as he went, for it is a teaching that ought to be held by everyone. Even this faith or belief, if it went no further, would produce some effects. Yet unless it produced fine works, it would be valueless and would not lead to salvation. James proves his point when he next says:

20 But do you care to know, O empty man, that faith apart from works is inactive?

And yet the demons believe and shudder

Here James shows that mere belief in itself is not genuine faith, even though it may have some emotional effects. The demons, spirit creatures, angels disobedient to God, have actually seen God and know that he exists, and that he is one God. Their knowledge of and belief in this fact have effects on them—they shudder, knowing that they are sentenced to destruction. (Mark 1:24; 2 Pet. 2:4; Jude 6) But certainly they will not be saved, for not only do they perform no good works, but their efforts are all works *against* God. So would anyone say to the demons, Your belief in God is enough, without good works; it will save you? It is of interest to note that none of the spirit creatures, not even demons, are atheists or agnostics. Atheism and agnosticism are doctrines found only on earth, among those who say that they would have to see God with their literal eyes to believe or to have faith in him.

20 But do you care to know, O empty man

Such a man has not filled himself with the true knowledge of God or his Word. (Jas. 1:18, 21) His heart, where real faith ought to reside, is empty, because such faith is nonexistent there.

that faith apart from works is inactive?

The "faith," or belief, such as demons possess produced something, namely, alarm, shuddering, in the demons. But as to any effectiveness toward salvation, it was absolutely inactive, barren.

21 Was not Abraham our father declared righteous
by works after he had offered up Isaac his son
upon the altar?

---

21 Was not Abraham our father

Abraham was the ancestor or progenitor of the
Jewish nation, of which James was a natural
member. However, James is not writing to the
Jews as a nation. He is addressing the scattered
Christians, from both Jewish and Gentile stock.
Nonetheless, Abraham was "the father of all
those having faith," both Jews and Gentiles. (Rom.
4:11, 12; compare 1 Peter 3:6, where Christian
women who have a spirit like that of Abraham's
wife Sarah are spoken of as "her children.")

declared righteous by works after he had offered up Isaac his son upon the altar?

Again, James does not argue contrary to Paul's

teaching. At Romans 4:2, 3, Paul writes that if Abraham "were declared righteous as a result of works, he would have ground for boasting; but not with God. For what does the scripture say? 'Abraham exercised faith in Jehovah, and it was counted to him as righteousness.'" Paul thus quotes the same scripture from Genesis 15:6 that James refers to later in verse 23 of the chapter of his letter that we are now considering. The words there contained were spoken of Abraham likely some 35 years before his act of attempting to offer up his son Isaac, the event to which James refers. How, then, do the inspired writings of Paul and James harmonize?

Genesis 15:1-6 shows that Abraham was declared righteous by faith when he believed God's promise to make his seed like the stars of heaven for number, this at a time when there was no tangible evidence that Abraham would have a child, since Sarah had long been barren. Why, then, can James state that Abraham was "declared righteous by works"? Because God later gave a *pronouncement* or *verdict of righteousness* to Abraham as a result of or out of his works, when he offered Isaac. By this act Abraham *proved*, demonstrated beyond question, that his original faith in God and in his power had been, and still was, genuine. He proved that his faith was a living faith, not a dead one. It was not Abraham's works of themselves that brought righteousness to him, but his works were a product of that genuine faith that he had, and God, by his verdict, affirmed this fact. Abraham's willingness to obey God's command to sacrifice his son was an outstanding point at which to make the pronouncement of Genesis 22:12.

22 You behold that his faith worked along with
his works and by his works his faith was perfected,

**22 You behold that his faith worked along with
his works and by his works his faith was
perfected**

Abraham's faith helped him, motivated him to
do good works. We may note that James does not
say that Abraham had works alone, but he states
that "his faith worked along with his works."
Abraham would never have attempted to offer
up his son if he had not had faith. At the same
time, if he had not *obeyed* God's command, he
would not have gained God's decree of approval.
God then would never have given confirmation of
Abraham's faith and his justification by faith.
So, both faith and works contributed to the result, not faith alone, nor works alone.

God knew that Abraham fully believed when
the promise, as recorded at Genesis 12:1-3, was
first given. And God could foresee that Abraham's
faith would certainly motivate him to works of
obedience. Abraham's works, performed before
God and men, justified God's confidence in him
that had been expressed years beforehand, and
led to God's confirmation of it. Consider God's
words after Abraham had demonstrated his faith
by works. God said: "Now I do know [or, recognize, acknowledge] that you are God-fearing in
that you have not withheld your son, your only
one, from me." (Gen. 22:12)

That Abraham was viewed by God as a righteous man was demonstrated even before Isaac's
birth, when God said: "Abraham is surely going
to become a nation great and mighty, and all the
nations of the earth must bless themselves by

23 and the scripture was fulfilled which says: "Abraham put faith in Jehovah, and it was counted to him as righteousness," and he came to be called "Jehovah's friend."

---

means of him. For I have become acquainted with him in order that he may command his sons and his household after him so that they shall keep Jehovah's way to do righteousness and judgment; in order that Jehovah may certainly bring upon Abraham what he has spoken about him." (Gen. 18:18, 19) So, Abraham's faith was "perfected," or "completed," not in the sense that it needed something, that it was lacking or inadequate in the first place, for it was not imperfect in itself. (Compare the reference to Jesus' being made perfect at Hebrews 2:10.) Rather, God, by dealing with Abraham and by His command to him, brought forth works from Abraham to the point of a complete test of Abraham's faith. Abraham's faith, combined with works, led to the attaining of the objective of his faith.

23 and the scripture was fulfilled which says: "Abraham put faith in Jehovah, and it was counted to him as righteousness"

James here quotes Genesis 15:6. As we have seen, long before Isaac's birth Jehovah had promised Abraham that his seed would become as numerous as the stars of heaven. (Gen. 15:5) When Abraham attempted to offer up Isaac, it appeared that this promise would be made void because without a living Isaac the promise could not be fulfilled. (God had said: "It is by means of Isaac that what will be called your seed will be." [Gen. 21:12]) Abraham's faith moved him to obey God's command to sacrifice Isaac, for "he reckoned that God was able to raise him up even from the dead; and from there he did receive him also in an illustrative way." (Heb. 11:19) So the scripture at Genesis 15:6 stating that Abraham was declared righteous because of his faith was "fulfilled." How? In that now that first declaration of righteousness was clearly shown to have been a right and properly made declaration. What demonstrated it to be such? Abraham's works, his willing obedience to God's command regarding his son. God's act in initially declaring Abraham righteous through his faith was now shown to be justified, soundly based. He had read Abraham's heart correctly as Abraham's obedience in this severe test showed. And so, at the time of Abraham's attempted sacrifice of Isaac, God reaffirmed what he had earlier stated and went further, sealing his promise with an oath. (Heb. 6:13-17) Abraham's faith brought him to this complete confirmation of the promise, because it was a genuine faith that prompted works. Knowing that Abraham had this faith, God led him to do works proving it beyond question. If Abraham had not obeyed in offering Isaac, his faith would have been inoperative, valueless.

James thus makes a strong argument indeed that faith that is of real, genuine worth will have works as evidence. And what works it prompted Abraham to do! Hence, the answer is Yes to the question raised in James 2:21: "Was not Abraham our father declared righteous by works after he had offered up Isaac his son upon the altar?" He was declared righteous years beforehand. But Abraham's works *confirmed* the pronouncement that God had made years earlier, and God at this point *acknowledged* his initial declaration. Thus, James is destroying the argument of those who

24 You see that a man is to be declared righteous
by works, and not by faith alone.

---

imagined that they had faith, though they had no
works as evidence.

and he came to be called "Jehovah's friend"

Abraham's works proved that he had deep,
heartfelt faith, and that he truly loved God. He
demonstrated before God and men that he was,
in word and deed, a friend of God, so that King
Jehoshaphat could refer to him as God's "lover,"
and Jehovah could say, through the prophet
Isaiah: "You, O Israel, are my servant, you, O
Jacob, whom I have chosen, the seed of Abraham
my friend." (2 Chron. 20:7, NW; Rotherham;
Isa. 41:8) The Hebrew word translated "friend"
at Isaiah 41:8 is the same as the word rendered
"lover" in 2 Chronicles 20:7; and there King
Jehoshaphat declares Abraham to be the "lover"
or "friend" of God. (NW, margin, 1958 edition)
It was later that Jehovah, through Isaiah, spoke
of Abraham as "my friend" or "lover" (NW;
Rotherham)

24 You see that a man is to be declared righteous by works, and not by faith alone

This proof that has just been presented in the
case of one of the most outstanding servants of
God should enable us to "see" that a claim of
faith, with no works to show for it, is ineffective
and worthless and leads to no justification or the
declaring of a person righteous. If Christians
claimed to believe in the "good news" but never
did anything in connection with such belief—if
they never spoke about God and Christ and the
"good news" to others, if they never did anything

25 In the same manner was not also Rahab the harlot declared righteous by works, after she had received the messengers hospitably and sent them out by another way?

---

to help another person, if their claimed faith never made any change in their lives for the better, of what worth would Christianity be?

God, who searches the heart, knows whether faith is real or not, and he declares a person righteous on the basis of genuine faith. But a faith that does not produce good works is merely a speculative or imagined faith. A person with such "faith" would not be accepted by God from the very start—he would not be declared righteous, because God would know in advance that his imagined faith would not produce good works. (Consider God's foreknowledge of Saul [Paul], Jacob, John the Baptist and Jeremiah [Gal. 1:15; Gen. 25:23; Luke 1:15-17; Jer. 1:5].)

25 In the same manner was not also Rahab the harlot declared righteous by works, after she

had received the messengers hospitably and sent them out by another way?

Rahab had been, up to that time in her life, a harlot. James apparently uses this illustration to show that true faith results in immediate good works, even a direct about-face in one's activities. It can cause one to take a definite stand for God and his people, completely forsaking a former way of life. (Acts 3:19)

Rahab had faith *before* she performed works. The apostle Paul says: "By faith Rahab the harlot did not perish with those who acted disobediently, because she received the spies in a peaceable way." (Heb. 11:31) Rahab spoke of the things that she had heard about Jehovah's leading the Israelites, and added: "I do know that Jehovah will certainly give you the land . . . For we have heard how Jehovah dried up the waters of the Red Sea . . . When we got to hear it, then our hearts began to melt, and no spirit has arisen yet in anybody because of you, for Jehovah your God is God in the heavens above and on the earth beneath." (Josh. 2:9-11) She recognized Jehovah as the God deserving of her worship before she met the spies. Her subsequent words revealed her faith, that God would give the land to Israel and, furthermore, he could and would protect her from destruction with Jericho if she acted in behalf of the two Israelite spies.

Rahab's was no inactive, barren faith. God would certainly not have declared her righteous if she had possessed only a sham, unproductive faith, and had not taken steps to protect the spies, but had allowed these representatives of the God of Israel to be killed. Rahab later married the Judean Israelite Salmon, and became an ancestress of Jesus Christ. (Matt. 1:5-16)

26 Indeed, as the body without spirit is dead, so
also faith without works is dead.

---

26 Indeed, as the body without spirit is dead, so also faith without works is dead

When a man is dead, there is no animating force or "spirit." So there is no work produced. Anyone can see this, and can be sure that there is no "spirit" in the body. The corpse is good for nothing, but must be buried out of sight. Likewise, a merely professed faith is as lifeless, unproductive and useless as a dead body. Faith cannot be seen by the literal eye as one can see a person, but works of faith can be seen. Where there is no animation in a person, *no moving to good works,* this is conclusive evidence that no living faith exists in him, for faith is a motivating force just as "spirit," or, life force, is motivating for the body. On the other hand, where Christian works abound, evidence abounds that faith is there motivating the individual to right works. So James concludes his argument with an illustration that could hardly have been more appropriate.

QUESTIONS FOR STUDY

VERSE 1

My brothers
1 How can James call his readers "brothers" when they were displaying some wrong attitudes?

you are not holding the faith
1 Why did James say that the brothers were not holding the faith?

of our Lord Jesus Christ, our glory
1 In what way may Jesus Christ be called "our glory"?
2 What counsel does the reference to the glorious Lord emphasize?

with acts of favoritism, are you?
1 Why is it a notable sin to show favoritism?

2 At Leviticus 19:15, what two aspects of favoritism were prohibited by the Law?

VERSE 2

For, if a man with gold rings on his fingers and in splendid clothing enters into a gathering of you
1 Who was the man about whom James here spoke?

but a poor man in filthy clothing also enters
1 Who was the poor man here referred to?

VERSE 3

yet you look with favor upon the one wearing the splendid clothing and say: "You take this seat here in a fine place"
1 Was James here saying that courtesy ought not to be shown to the rich, ostentatious man, or what?

and you say to the poor one: "You keep standing," or: "Take that seat there under my footstool"
1 In what way was the congregation treating the poor man?

VERSE 4

You have class distinctions among yourselves
1 How was the congregation, by its partiality, going contrary to the spirit of Christ?
2 How can it be shown that they had serious flaws in their faith?

and you have become judges rendering wicked decisions, is that not so?
1 On what grounds were the partial ones making their judgments?
2 In what way were they "judges rendering wicked decisions"?
3 How did they, by their wicked judgments, disrespect the "Lord Jesus Christ, our glory"?

VERSE 5

Listen, my beloved brothers
1 Why did James write: "Listen" and call his readers "my beloved brothers"?

God chose the ones who are poor respecting the world
1 Does God choose people merely because they are poor?
2 Why is it that rich and influential persons are often not interested in hearing the "good news"?
3 Why has it usually been true that poor persons are more ready to listen to the "good news"?

to be rich in faith and heirs of the kingdom

1 What does James mean by the expression "rich in faith"?

2 Those "rich in faith" are heirs of what?

which he promised to those who love him, did he not?

1 Do those who receive the Kingdom initially have this strong love for God?

2 How do they come to have and develop this love?

VERSE 6

You, though, have dishonored the poor man

1 How were these brothers 'dishonoring' the poor man?

The rich oppress you, and they drag you before law courts, do they not?

1 How were the rich often the chief persecutors of Christians? Give examples.

2 Does this mean that the poor never became opposers of Christians?

VERSE 7

They blaspheme the fine name by which you were called, do they not?

1 What is blasphemy?

2 How were the rich oppressors blaspheming the name by which the congregation was called?

VERSE 8

If, now, you practice carrying out the kingly law according to the scripture: "You must love your neighbor as yourself," you are doing quite well

1 Why is the law (found at Leviticus 19:18) the "kingly law"?

2 How was the congregation "doing quite well"?

VERSE 9

But if you continue showing favoritism, you are working a sin

1 If a Christian shows kind attention to a rich man, is he doing wrong?

2 In what way will he show himself to be really following the "kingly law"?

for you are reproved by the law as transgressors

1 How is the person showing favoritism reproved by the "kingly law" as a transgressor?

2 What must Christians get away from in order to show themselves followers of the "kingly law"?

VERSE 10

For whoever observes all the Law but makes a false step in one point

1 Whom is James here reproving?
2 What is the tendency of humans toward any set of laws?

he has become an offender against them all
1 How is the breaker of one of the laws "an offender against them all"?
2 In worldly courts, does the keeping of all other laws excuse the person who violates one specific law?
3 Show that it is true that one trying to keep the Mosaic law had to keep it *all* to be righteous.
4 How only can a person be forgiven of his sins and become free from condemnation?

VERSE 11

For he who said: "You must not commit adultery," said also: "You must not murder"
1 Why did James evidently here choose to cite the laws on adultery and murder?

If, now, you do not commit adultery but you do murder, you have become a transgressor of law
1 Why would one breaking one point of the Law be a transgressor against all of it?

VERSE 12

Keep on speaking in such a way and keep on doing in such a way as those do who are going to be judged by the law of a free people
1 What is "the law of a free people," and what advantage comes to those under it?
2 Does "the law of a free people" give such people freedom to live according to their own inclinations?
3 On what basis can the "free people" be forgiven their sins?
4 Therefore, how do spiritual Israelites conduct themselves?

VERSE 13

For the one that does not practice mercy will have his judgment without mercy
1 What is in store for those who practice favoritism?
2 How could the Christians to whom James wrote be inconsistent by their practice of partiality?

Mercy exults triumphantly over judgment
1 Under the "law of freedom," what advantage does the merciful man have who comes into a position in which he is being judged?
2 Give illustrations of this principle.

VERSE 14

Of what benefit is it, my brothers, if a certain one says he has faith but he does not have works?

1 Does James fully agree with the apostle Paul on the teaching of justification by faith and not by works of law?
2 Why, then, does James take up this subject of faith and works?
3 What kind of man is one who says he has faith but does not have works?
4 How did Jesus show that a mere profession of faith is not enough?
5 How do James' words here harmonize with his words in chapter 1:26, 27?

That faith cannot save him, can it?

1 What is shown by the expression *"that* faith"?
2 Describe the works that Paul is talking about as compared with the works that James discusses.
3 Did Paul believe that genuine faith would unquestionably produce works?

VERSES 15, 16

If a brother or a sister is in a naked state and lacking the food sufficient for the day, yet a certain one of you says to them: "Go in peace, keep warm and well fed," but you do not give them the necessities for their body, of what benefit is it?

1 What point is James illustrating by these verses?
2 What did Job have to say about this?

VERSE 17

Thus, too, faith, if it does not have works, is dead in itself

1 Why is faith without works dead?
2 How is such faith dead "according to itself"?

VERSE 18

Nevertheless, a certain one will say: "You have faith, and I have works. Show me your faith apart from the works, and I shall show you my faith by my works"

1 How may the argument presented by the "certain one" be understood?
2 What proves that a person possesses genuine faith?

VERSE 19

You believe there is one God, do you? You are doing quite well

    1 If a person only went so far as to believe that there is one God, why would he be doing well?

    2 Though this belief is certainly true, would this by itself lead to salvation?

And yet the demons believe and shudder

    1 Do the demons believe that there is one true God?

    2 Why will such belief or "faith" not save them?

    3 Where only do we find the doctrines of atheism or agnosticism?

VERSE 20

But do you care to know, O empty man

    1 Why is a person an "empty man" who believes that faith without works will save him?

that faith apart from works is inactive?

    1 What does the "faith" that the demons have, that there is one God, do for them?

VERSE 21

Was not Abraham our father

    1 Why did James, writing to Christians, call Abraham "our father"?

declared righteous by works after he had offered up Isaac his son upon the altar?

    1 In referring to the same scripture James quoted, what does Paul say as to the basis for Abraham's being declared righteous?

    2 Likely how long before Abraham's attempted sacrifice of Isaac were the words in Genesis 15:6 spoken, and, hence, when was Abraham declared righteous by faith?

    3 Why, then, does James say that Abraham was declared righteous by works, likely some 35 years later?

VERSE 22

You behold that his faith worked along with his works and by his works his faith was perfected

    1 How do James' words here show that Abraham had faith first, then works as a result of faith?

    2 Was God's statement at Genesis 22:12 an initial declaration of righteousness for Abraham, or what?

    3 What did God know about Abraham at the time that He made the promise at Genesis 12:1-3?

    4 How, then, did Abraham's works 'perfect' his faith?

VERSE 23

and the scripture was fulfilled which says: "Abraham

put faith in Jehovah, and it was counted to him as righteousness"

1 When God commanded Abraham to sacrifice his son, how did Abraham demonstrate that he had possessed faith in God all along—all the years from the promise at Genesis 15:5?

2 How was the scripture at Genesis 15:6 thereby "fulfilled"?

3 On what basis was Abraham declared righteous by God?

4 Why does James present this argument?

and he came to be called "Jehovah's friend"

1 How was Abraham rightly called "Jehovah's friend"?

VERSE 24

You see that a man is to be declared righteous by works, and not by faith alone

1 What should we learn from James' presentation of the illustration concerning Abraham?

2 Why would God not declare righteous the person who has a "faith" that God knows will not produce works?

VERSE 25

In the same manner was not also Rahab the harlot declared righteous by works, after she had received the messengers hospitably and sent them out by another way?

1 What fact about faith is illustrated in the account about Rahab?

2 When did Rahab have faith—before or after her works?

3 On the basis of which was Rahab declared righteous—her faith or her works?

4 Why, then, does James say that Rahab was declared righteous by works?

5 If Rahab had not helped the Israelite spies, but had left them in danger of capture, would her knowledge that God had given Israel victories over Egypt and other nations have been real *faith?*

VERSE 26

Indeed, as the body without spirit is dead, so also faith without works is dead

1 How can faith without works well be compared to a dead body?

2 On the other hand, how do Christian works give evidence of a living faith?

CHAPTER 3

1 Not many of you should become teachers, my brothers, knowing that we shall receive heavier judgment.

---

1 Not many of you should become teachers, my brothers

This portion of James' letter is one that should prompt serious thought in those who would serve as teachers in the Christian congregation, as it points out their weighty responsibility and accountability to God.

Weighty Responsibility Resting upon Teachers

Was James' counsel here a discouraging of those who sincerely desired to serve as teachers of others? Obviously not. Hebrews 5:12-14 shows that, in course of time, all Christians should be sharing in teaching others the vital truths of God's Word. (Compare Titus 2:3; Acts 18:24-26.) But in addition to such teaching in a general sense, those who 'reached out' for the "fine work" of serving as overseers and shepherds in the congregations were to meet the requirement of being "qualified to teach." (1 Tim. 3:1, 2; compare 1 Timothy 5:17; Titus 1:5, 9.) On such a congregational level, only the brothers, the men, could serve as teachers. The apostle Paul says: "I do not permit a woman to teach [referring here to teaching the congregation], or to exercise authority over a man, but to be in silence." (1 Tim. 2:12)

Additionally, the Scriptures show that among Christians there were varieties of abilities and services, and some had special ability in the field of teaching, serving notably in that way. (Compare Romans 12:3-8; 1 Corinthians 12:4-11, 29.) This was clearly true even among congregational

99

elders. In fleshly Israel, among Jewish elders there were those who were esteemed as teachers of God's law, there being some in all the villages. (Luke 2:46; 5:17; John 3:9, 10; Acts 5:34; 22:3) In spiritual Israel, after Pentecost the 12 apostles initially served as a teaching body on behalf of the newly formed Christian congregation. (Acts 2:42; 6:2-4) The apostle Paul later states that, just as some of those whom Christ gave as "gifts in men" served as apostles and others as prophets and evangelizers, some also served as "shepherds and teachers," all contributing to a common goal. (Eph. 4:8, 11-16) At Acts 13:1 we read that "in Antioch there were prophets and teachers in the local congregation." Since all elders taught, it seems obvious that these "teachers" were notably capable and active in this field. (Compare Acts 15:35; 1 Timothy 4:13-16.) Paul speaks of himself as serving in three capacities, as "preacher and apostle and teacher." (2 Tim. 1:11; 1 Tim. 2:7)

In view of these facts, wherein lay the problem? As shown subsequently, James stresses the point that those becoming teachers will come under a heavier judgment, and this is so because of their liability to stumbling in word. The danger, therefore, lay in some seeking to act in the capacity of teachers who, though perhaps sincere, were not genuinely qualified to do so. This would be to the spiritual injury of the congregation. Worse, some might be motivated by pride and ambition and thrust themselves forward, seeking to gain influence and prominence as teachers. That self-confidence did indeed lead to such a pitfall for some is seen by such texts as Romans 2:17-21; 1 Timothy 6:2-4.

There can be no doubt as to the attraction this might have been for some among "the twelve tribes that are scattered about," spiritual Israelites, to whom James wrote. (Jas. 1:1) Similar to the power that a governmental ruler exercises, one highly regarded as a teacher among the Jews exercised powerful influence. The title "Rabbi" was applied to such, and John said this meant "teacher."* (John 1:38; compare John 3:2.) The Bible shows the prominence, exaltation and favor the Jewish rabbis often sought and gained through such standing. (Matt. 23:6, 7) Therefore, just as Jesus counseled his disciples on the need to avoid the ambitious desire for preeminence like that of earthly rulers, he also warned: "But you, do not you be called Rabbi, for one is your teacher, whereas all you are brothers." (Matt. 23:8-12; compare Luke 22:25, 26.)

The need for James' counsel is borne out by Paul's words to Timothy at 1 Timothy 1:3-7, instructing him to "command certain ones not to teach different doctrine, nor to pay attention to false stories and to genealogies, which end up in nothing, but which furnish questions for research." Hence, Paul went on to say: "Really the objective of this mandate is love out of a clean heart and out of a good conscience and out of faith without hypocrisy. By deviating from these things certain ones have been turned aside into idle talk, wanting to be teachers of law, but not perceiving either the things they are saying or the things about which they are making strong assertions." Such "teachers of law" were very dogmatic and doubtless often impressed their listeners with their self-confidence and persistence. But if carefully examined in the light of the whole Word of God, in harmony with Acts 17:11, they were seen to be sham, or false, teachers. (Compare Acts 15:1; 2 Corinthians 11:5, 12, 13; 2 Timothy 4:1-4.)

In view of the heaviness of the responsibility,

---

* Literally, "Rabbi" means "My great one; My excellent one."

therefore, anyone desiring to serve as a congregational teacher should carefully examine his motives and humbly assess his qualifications. (Rom. 12:3, 16) He should realize that not merely knowledge and ability but also real spirituality and a love for God, his Word and for the brothers are vital requirements. (1 Cor. 13:1, 2, 4; 14:6, 26) In this, as in all matters, rather than recommending himself, he should let others recommend him. (2 Cor. 10:12, 18; compare Proverbs 25:27; 27:2.)

knowing that we shall receive heavier judgment

Because a teacher stands before others as instructing or leading them, more is required of him. His life should be exemplary. (Compare Romans 2:21-24.) He comes under closer scrutiny than do other members of the congregation. This is in harmony with the Scriptural principle: "Everyone to whom much was given, much will be demanded of him; and the one whom people put in charge of much, they will demand more than usual of him." (Luke 12:48) Members of the congregation expect more from a teacher than they do from others, as they logically should. Also, by reason of his serious responsibility toward fellow believers, a teacher has a heavier account to render. His influence is more far reaching for good or for harm. God judges him accordingly. By saying "we," James includes himself as being under the same responsibility toward the impartial Judge.

If a man errs in his teaching and this results in problems for members of the congregation, he will be judged by Jehovah God through the Lord Jesus Christ. Jesus said: "I tell you that every unprofitable saying that men speak, they will render an account concerning it on Judgment Day; for by your words you will be declared righteous, and by your words you will be condemned." (Matt. 12:36, 37) What a person teaches will

2 For we all stumble many times. If anyone does not stumble in word, this one is a perfect man, able to bridle also his whole body.

---

have a heavy bearing on the reward that he receives. (Matt. 16:27; 2 Cor. 5:10) There is therefore need for care, study, humility, modesty and a deep sense of a Christian teacher's responsibility to hold faithfully to God's Word.

2 For we all stumble many times

Humbly, James includes himself among his fellow believers as being prone to stumble while following the Christian course of life. Because of sinful inclinations and imperfections all persons, *including teachers*, have shortcomings. (Rom. 7:19-23; 1 John 1:8) This is a sobering thought. One of the most frequent ways, one which at times can be most damaging, is stumbling in word. This danger should make a person very cautious about the instruction he gives. Bible commentator J. H. Ropes was moved to remark: "The profession of teaching is the most difficult mode of life conceivable."*

Even exemplary teachers are prone to stumble; how much greater is the peril in the case of men who are unqualified. Since all stumbling in word can injure others, the more any teacher may err, the more harm will result to the whole congregation.

If anyone does not stumble in word, this one is a perfect man

The man who can keep his speech completely in check and does not err with his lips is perfect. If he is able to stop himself from expressing wrong

---

* *The International Critical Commentary,* page 225 (on The Letter of James).

3 If we put bridles in the mouths of horses for them to obey us, we manage also their whole body.

---

views, feelings, emotions and passions, then such a man has complete, perfect control of himself. As James notes in this verse, no one of imperfect humankind can do this, for "we all stumble many times." Only Jesus Christ, the perfect man, had complete control of his tongue. (Heb. 7:26) Christians can do their best, however, to come as near as possible to this goal. They know that they cannot accomplish this in their own strength and, as God's witnesses, they certainly cannot remain entirely silent. But they rely on God's spirit and meditate on the good things his Word counsels. They try to keep their minds on "whatever things are true, whatever things are of serious concern . . . righteous . . . chaste . . . lovable . . . well spoken of, whatever virtue there is and whatever praiseworthy thing there is." (Phil. 4:8) They trust in the holy spirit to help them to bring "every thought into captivity to make it obedient to the Christ," for they know that "out of the heart's abundance [a man's] mouth speaks." (2 Cor. 10:5; Luke 6:45; compare Matthew 15:18-20.)

able to bridle also his whole body

The tongue is the member of the body that, among humankind, has generally caused the most trouble. Hence, James says that the man able to bridle it should also be able to control the other members of his body.

3 If we put bridles in the mouths of horses for them to obey us, we manage also their whole body

This is an illustration showing that the ability to control the tongue is related to the ability to

4 Look! Even boats, although they are so big and are driven by hard winds, are steered by a very small rudder to where the inclination of the man at the helm wishes.

---

manage the entire body. By means of small bridles, with their bits in the mouths of horses, men can manage these powerful animals, even high-spirited ones, causing them to move in the desired direction. A firm grip on the reins attached to the bridle is, of course, essential. Humans similarly can control the other parts of their bodies, with their propensities to sin, if they control the tongue. To the extent imperfection allows, they should work hard to do this.

4 Look! Even boats, although they are so big

This illustration makes a similar point, but this time more markedly emphasizes difference in size. A boat is tremendously larger than its rudder, which James goes on to mention. Evidently, in keeping with the principle of the Mosaic law that every matter be established at the mouth

5 So, too, the tongue is a little member and yet makes great brags. Look! How little a fire it takes to set so great a woodland on fire!

---

of at least two witnesses, James used two illustrations to confirm and to clarify his statement about being able to manage the whole body if a person had perfect control of the tongue. (2 Cor. 13:1; Deut. 17:6)

and are driven by hard winds, are steered by a very small rudder to where the inclination of the man at the helm wishes

A ship is subject to the force of strong winds and waves. Yet it is not those powerful forces, but the position of the rudder, as manipulated by the man at the helm, that determines the ship's course. Thus the small rudder, moved by the firm grip of the helmsman's hand, exerts control over the entire ship. Though the ship is affected by mighty forces of sea and wind, the comparatively minute rudder can be used and controlled to offset these forces.

5 So, too, the tongue is a little member

As the bridle is small compared to the horse, and the rudder compared to the ship, so with the tongue. Compared with the entire human body, the tongue is a very small member. As we consider what James says about the tongue we need to keep in mind that what is said applies with double force to those who are, or who aspire to be, *teachers,* for James here especially has teachers in mind.

The Power of the Tongue

and yet makes great brags

The tongue can actually accomplish great good if used aright. "Death and life are in the power

6 Well, the tongue is a fire. The tongue is constituted a world of unrighteousness among our members, for it spots up all the body and sets the wheel of natural life aflame and it is set aflame by Gehenna.

---

of the tongue, and he that is loving it will eat its fruitage." (Prov. 18:21; 25:15) But when its owner lets it loose, it can do much harm, first of all to him, and then to others. (Prov. 10:14; 17:4, 20; 21:6) The tongue often makes its presence and influence felt by great brags, and indeed it can "brag" that it does exert much power for good or for bad, though such bragging is unchristian. The psalmist wrote about such action of the tongue: "Jehovah will cut off . . . the tongue speaking great things, those who have said: 'With our tongue we shall prevail.'" (Ps. 12:3, 4) The tongue of such men was indeed boasting, being used in voicing self-confidence. These wicked men, who were afflicting lowly ones in Israel, had no faith in God and the working of his judgment. They believed that, through the words formed by their tongue, they would attain their evil ends with impunity.

Look! How little a fire it takes to set so great a woodland on fire

Just a tiny spark may be enough to set an entire forest aflame. Having illustrated the power a small unit can exercise over something far larger than itself, James now focuses on the hurtful effects of failing to control a little thing. He here uses a new illustration, of an uncontrolled fire, to emphasize the widespread devastation caused by an uncontrolled tongue.

6 Well, the tongue is a fire

In having the capacity for causing untold damage, the unbridled tongue is hard to match. It is, in this case, set off, not by calmness and reason, but by impulse, anger, hate, and so forth. (Compare Isaiah 9:18.)

The tongue is constituted a world of unrighteousness among our members

Among the members of the human body, the uncontrolled tongue is in itself a world of unrighteousness. All the evil of the world alienated from God can be seen in the unbridled tongue. Through slander, scandal, false testimony, misrepresentation, reviling, deceptive propaganda and erroneous teaching, the tongue has been responsible for a multitude of crimes. (Compare Matthew 15:11, 18-20.) It has been used even to make unrighteous, lawless things appear to be beautiful or beneficial. "Woe to those who are saying that good is bad and bad is good, those who are putting darkness for light and light for darkness, those who are putting bitter for sweet and sweet for bitter!" (Isa. 5:20; Rom. 16:18; 2 Cor. 11:13, 14; 2 Pet. 2:3) Why, there is no form of unrighteousness to which the wicked tongue cannot give origin or momentum.

for it spots up all the body

The person who misuses his tongue "spots up" or defiles his entire body, and, in the process, his whole self. What he says reveals what he is as a person. The man repeatedly caught in lying, for example, shows himself to be morally defective, untrustworthy. His whole being, not just his tongue, comes to have the designation "liar" attached to it. Rash talk, or words spoken without due consideration, cause a man to be labeled as unreliable. "Have you beheld a man hasty with his words? There is more hope for someone stupid than for him." (Prov. 29:20) To avoid such stains on us as persons, we must work at control of the tongue.

and sets the wheel of natural life aflame

In the original Greek, the expression "wheel of natural life" is, literally, "wheel of the birth." The unbridled tongue can set aflame the whole round or course of natural life into which a person came by birth, making life become like a vicious circle, possibly even resulting in its own destruction as if by fire. (Eccl. 10:12, 13) Not only this, but it also may affect his associates. (Prov. 11:9) If he misuses his tongue as he continues in his life course, he radiates harmfulness and may do much injury to those who come in contact with him. (Prov. 16:28; 6:12) For example, an entire congregation, or more than one congregation of God's people, may be defiled by one person with an uncontrolled tongue. (Heb. 12:15; Gal. 5:9; compare Ecclesiastes 9:18.)

and it is set aflame by Gehenna

The expression "Gehenna" is drawn from two Hebrew words, *Ga'i* and *Hinnom*, meaning Valley of Hinnom. (Jer. 19:2, 6) This valley, situated south and southwest of Jerusalem, was the scene of child sacrifice in the days of Judean kings Ahaz and Manasseh. (2 Chron. 28:1-3; 33:1, 6; Jer. 7:31) Later, faithful King Josiah made the valley unfit for such abominable worship. (2 Ki. 23:10) According to Jewish tradition, it became a place for the disposal of the city's refuse by fire.

That Gehenna should be associated with the destructive aspects of a city dump is also confirmed by Jesus Christ. Regarding Gehenna, he said: "Their maggot does not die and the fire is not put out." (Mark 9:48) This suggests that the fires burned continually at the city dump, perhaps being intensified by the addition of sulfur. Wherever the flames did not reach, worms or maggots would breed and feed on the refuse that was not consumed by fire. Accordingly, Gehenna

7 For every species of wild beast as well as bird and creeping thing and sea creature is to be tamed and has been tamed by humankind.

---

is clearly an appropriate symbol of total annihilation. (Compare Isaiah 30:33; Jeremiah 19:6, 7.)

When misused, the tongue can be destructive like Gehenna, to the extent that it becomes an agent for Gehenna. It is as if Gehenna, symbolizing annihilation, has lent its destructive power to the tongue. Like a small torch that is lighted from a major fire and that can carry the destructive fire and spread it to other locations, so is the tongue. The person himself can also become a victim of the blaze that his own tongue has become. The sin that will never be forgiven—blasphemy against the holy spirit—is a sin of the tongue. (Matt. 12:31, 32) Jesus Christ said: "Whoever says, 'You despicable fool!' will be liable to the fiery Gehenna." (Matt. 5:22) The person who wrongly condemned his brother as a "despicable fool," that is, as being morally worthless, would be in great danger of such a serious consequence. This is because he would be viewing his brother as deserving the judgment of Gehenna, or hoping that his brother would suffer that judgment. In his heart he would be desiring this for his brother and, therefore, would be putting himself in line for the punishment he wished for the one whom he was calling a "despicable fool." (Compare Deuteronomy 19:16-21; 1 John 3:14, 15.)

7 For every species of wild beast

James is evidently speaking in a general sense as regards the taming (mentioned later in the verse) of these creatures. Nonetheless, man has succeeded in training all kinds of animals to accomplish certain feats. These animals include elephants, lions and tigers. Even today the per-

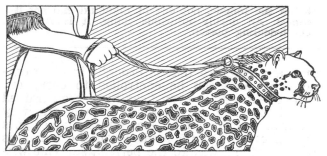

formances of wild beasts in circuses testify to man's ability to bring powerful wild beasts under his control. This is in harmony with God's original declaration that man should have the animal creation in subjection. (Gen. 1:28)

as well as bird

Not even birds, which are quick and swift-flying and very hard to catch, are exempted from man's control. For example, men have long used trained falcons, hawks and even eagles in hunting. The origin of this practice, known as falconry, is attributed to the ancient Persians.

and creeping thing

These may include serpents. However, the practice of snake charming may be a form of spiritism. (Ps. 58:4, 5; Eccl. 10:11; Jer. 8:17)

and sea creature

Though these live in a different element and are far different in makeup, aquatic animals, including crocodiles, whales and porpoises, are among the sea creatures that man has been able to control, even using some to do beneficial work.

is to be tamed and has been tamed by humankind

Seemingly, with time, patience and persever-

8 But the tongue, not one of mankind can get it tamed. An unruly injurious thing, it is full of death-dealing poison.

---

ance, any creature that is brought in close contact with man can be controlled to carry out certain feats. Why, even fleas have been trained to pull tiny wagons. All these animals give way to man's superior intelligence but, as James goes on to show, the sinful tendency of the tongue is to resist giving way to the perfect, supreme wisdom of God.

8 But the tongue, not one of mankind can get it tamed

While successful in getting mastery over all kinds of creatures, including ferocious beasts and poisonous serpents, sinful man has not been able to achieve perfect tongue control. He has mastered animals, but cannot master his tongue. His exercise of dominion is faulty.

An unruly injurious thing, it is full of death-dealing poison

The tongue is "unruly," "unsettled" (*Kingdom Interlinear Translation*). Sin inherited from Adam has unsettled the tongue, making it restless, unruly. It will not "settle down" to be controlled. Such a thing did not happen to the animal world. Hence, animals respond normally to men's efforts to tame them, while the tongue does not. A tongue that cannot be restrained but that becomes the instrument for making cutting, abusive or slanderous remarks, or that misleads by its teaching, is truly unruly and injurious. Since no one can fully prevent the tongue from doing these bad things, it requires the most diligent awareness, watchfulness and effort on the part of not

9 With it we bless Jehovah, even the Father, and yet with it we curse men who have come into existence "in the likeness of God."

---

only teachers but *every* Christian; otherwise a person's tongue can bring him to ruin. Because of the tremendous harm that it can bring about, it can be a dangerous instrument filled with deadly poison. (Compare Psalm 140:3; Romans 3:13.) In fact, fights that result from unbridled speech are not infrequently responsible for the loss of human life.

Think of the untold suffering and the billions of deaths caused by the acceptance of the first lie, told by Satan in the Garden of Eden! (John 8:44) We have many other examples of the deaths of thousands of people because of the deception of the false prophets and other leaders of the people. (Jer. 23:13, 14, 19-22; 50:6, 7; Isa. 19:11-13) Bad counsel on the part of King Rehoboam's associates and rash, harsh language on his part caused the kingdom of Israel to split and led to many wars. (1 Ki. 12:8, 14, 16, 17) Deceptive leadership of the people of Israel led the nation into committing the greatest crime in history—the murder of the Son of God. Both the rulers and the people acted in ignorance, but the ignorance of the rulers was more culpable, because they were blinded by their selfish desire to maintain their wealth and power, while the people followed their misleading speech and counsel. (Acts 3:14-17; John 11:45-50; 12:9-11; Matt. 23:27, 28; 12:31, 32) False teachers in the early Christian congregation, and since, have turned many persons away from God. (1 Tim. 1:18-20; 4:1, 2; 2 Pet. 2:1-3) These things provide food for serious thought on the part of men who aspire to be teachers in the Christian congregation.

9 With it we bless Jehovah, even the Father, and yet with it we curse men who have come into existence "in the likeness of God"

In the physical sense, and as descendants of Adam, all persons owe their existence to Jehovah God as the original Life-Giver and Creator. In this sense He is the Progenitor, or Father, of all; and therefore the apostle Paul could say to a group of Athenians: "[God] himself gives to all persons life and breath and all things. And he made out of one man every nation of men . . . For by him we have life and move and exist . . . we are also his progeny." (Acts 17:22, 25-29) In a spiritual sense, he is the Father only of members of the true Christian congregation. These earnestly strive to imitate God and reflect his qualities, keeping separate from the world and the course of worldlings who manifest the qualities of God's adversary and who therefore bear the likeness of such adversary as their "father." (Compare James 1:27; John 1:11-13; 8:42-44; Ephesians 5:1; 1 John 3:10-12.)

On the one hand, then, James' counsel here given should have particular force for those within the true Christian congregation, those who are spiritual brothers. Nonetheless, in view of the inspired Scriptural teachings, the principle that James sets forth certainly is not restricted to the dealings a Christian has with his spiritual brothers, but applies to his dealings with all persons, fellow humans,

whoever they may be.—Compare Matthew 5:43-48.

Man was originally made in the likeness of God. (Gen. 1:26) This likeness of God pertains to his mental and moral qualities, not to his bodily appearance or structure. Such qualities, including love, justice and wisdom, distinguish humans from the animals. Though persons of the world may fail measurably in reflecting the likeness of their Creator, they still reflect this at least to some degree, even as they retain at least some measure of God-given conscience. (Compare Romans 2:13-15; Acts 28:1, 2.) Christians themselves cannot perfectly reflect the divine likeness and must humbly acknowledge that they also "fall short of the glory of God." (Rom. 3:23) But such failure, whether minor or major, never gives justification for dealing hatefully and abusively with others, arrogantly and disdainfully treating them as though they were from an inferior origin, different from that of oneself. The whole tenor of the Christian Scriptures is against such a prideful viewpoint. (Compare John 3:16; Romans 5:7, 8; Acts 10:28, 29.) The Pharisees were guilty of such an attitude and therefore disdained the common people of Israel, whom they viewed as sinners, calling them "accursed people." (John 7:49; Luke 18:9-14)

The tongue was, in fact, created primarily to bring praise to God. But sinful men may use the tongue inconsistently, blessing the Creator and then cursing his creation. To "curse" men means to 'invoke' or 'call down' evil upon them. It is true that the Scriptures record curses spoken by God's servants against men, and this with divine approval. It is clear, however, that such curses were made under divine inspiration and the evil invoked was brought to pass by divine power. (Compare Genesis 9:24, 25; 2 Kings 2:23, 24; Joshua 6:26; 1 Kings 16:34.) Thus, the apostle Peter, under inspiration, spoke words that resulted in the death of Ananias and Sapphira; and the apostle Paul invoked blindness upon the villainous opposer of the truth named Elymas, calling him an "enemy of everything righteous." (Acts 5:1-10; 13:6-11) In both cases it was by divine inspiration that the true heart motivations were discerned. Christians in general, however, were not endowed with the special apostolic powers that would enable them to make such direct pronouncements.

With regard to persons who might teach a so-called "good news" other than that which the apostles declared, the apostle Paul said: "Let [them] be accursed." (Gal. 1:8, 9; compare 2 Peter 2:14; 2 John 9-11.) But for Christians to view them as such was quite different from vocally expressing curses against them. Believers were exhorted to follow the example of the archangel Michael, who refrained from using abusive terms even toward God's adversary the Devil. (Jude 9) As regards all others, they had Christ's own injunction to "continue to love your enemies, to do good to those hating you, to bless those cursing you, to pray for those who are insulting you." (Luke 6:27, 28) And the apostle Paul wrote: "Keep on blessing those who persecute; be blessing and do not be cursing. Return evil for evil to no one. . . . Do not avenge yourselves, beloved, but yield place to the wrath; for it is written: 'Vengeance is mine; I will repay, says Jehovah' . . . keep conquering the evil with the good." (Rom. 12:14, 17-21)

So, when, without divine inspiration, the tongue is used in cursing men, any men, it really cannot be blessing God. Such words of blessing are shown up to be hypocritical. The apostle John made this clear when he wrote: "If anyone makes the statement: 'I love God,' and yet is hating his brother, he is a liar. For he who does not love his brother, whom he has seen, cannot be loving God, whom

10 Out of the same mouth come forth blessing and cursing.

It is not proper, my brothers, for these things to go on occurring this way.

---

he has not seen." (1 John 4:20) To pronounce a curse on someone (apart from divine inspiration) is certainly an evidence of hatred and not of love. Thus such cursing of men makes one's blessing of God vain. The Most High will never accept such as a genuine blessing.

Using the tongue wisely and properly now, or even most of the time, does not ensure against later misuse, with possible calamity to ourselves and others. Constant, unremitting vigilance is required. The most ready and ruinous expressions of the tongue are often triggered by anger. That is why the scripture warns: "Be wrathful, and yet do not sin." (Eph. 4:26)

10 Out of the same mouth come forth blessing and cursing

Since the tongue may be used for both blessing and cursing, two diametrically opposed things may come forth from the same mouth.

It is not proper, my brothers, for these things to go on occurring this way

In the case of Christians, especially, James says the speech organ should not be praising God and then cursing men made in God's likeness. Actually, we should not utter any curses except those that God has had recorded in the Bible, and then we cannot properly apply them to any individual, for we are not judges. Even in privacy with another, or in our own hearts, uttering a curse or pronouncement of evil against another is wrong. How contradictory it is for a person to attend Christian meetings, where he sings praises and speaks good things of God to his associates, and then to go out

11 A fountain does not cause the sweet and the bitter to bubble out of the same opening, does it?

---

and revile, slander or speak evil of his brothers! How utterly bad it is and what damage it does to one's standing with God!

Such cursing, as well as related wrongs such as backbiting, malicious gossip, vicious criticism, slander, would reveal the existence of a corrupt heart, for Jesus Christ said: "Out of the abundance of the heart the mouth speaks." (Matt. 12:34) For a Christian to use his tongue in such an inconsistent way is completely contrary to the purpose for which Jehovah God designed this organ of speech. It is something wholly improper. Such wicked use of the tongue is not only totally out of harmony with the divine will; it is also a gross incongruity.

11 A fountain does not cause the sweet and the bitter to bubble out of the same opening, does it?

The answer to this question, obviously, is, No. Water from a fountain can be either sweet or

12 My brothers, a fig tree cannot produce olives or a vine figs, can it? Neither can salt water produce sweet water.

---

bitter, but never can both sweet and bitter water bubble forth from the same opening. Such a contradictory thing is contrary to nature. Likewise, it is contrary to the natural laws of God for the mouth to be bubbling forth both good and bad speech. Only in humankind, whom sin has permeated, do we see something so unnatural, not in harmony with God's creation. How can God or man place reliance in a tongue that does these things? No more than a man would be willing to chance taking a drink from a spring producing sometimes good and sometimes bad water.

12 My brothers, a fig tree cannot produce olives or a vine figs, can it?

God's unchangeable law is that 'fruit trees yield according to their kinds.' (Gen. 1:11, 12) Though these fruits in themselves are good, the point James makes is that the tree or the vine would not be producing the fruit purposed, not what it was created to do. So this illustration again emphasizes the fact that misuse of the tongue is contrary to natural use or fitness.

Neither can salt water produce sweet water

While figs, olives and grapes are all good fruits, pleasant to the eater, one who desires sweet water and finds that it is salty is disappointed, and may be sickened. Here James again makes a contrast rather than a comparison. Salt water, not desired for drinking, will not change into sweet water. According to this principle, when the person who should bring forth good, tasty, satisfying words also persistently produces distasteful, sickening words, something is wrong.

13 Who is wise and understanding among you? Let him show out of his fine conduct his works with a mildness that belongs to wisdom.

He cannot be excused. (Compare 1 Timothy 6: 3-5.) Such contrary speech provides evidence that the source—the owner of the tongue—can sicken others. James uses all these examples to show that only in mankind, out of all physical creation, do these unnatural, contradictory things occur.

Logically, the fruitage of a person's mouth will agree with what he really is as a person. Jesus said: "Every good tree produces fine fruit, but every rotten tree produces worthless fruit; a good tree cannot bear worthless fruit, neither can a rotten tree produce fine fruit. Every tree not producing fine fruit gets cut down and thrown into the fire. Really, then, by their fruits you will recognize those men." (Matt. 7:17-20) Accordingly, the "fruits" we bear, including the fruit of our tongue, identify what we are, and there is great danger of being "cut down" if we use the tongue wrongly. This principle applies, in full force, to teachers in particular.

13 Who is wise and understanding among you?

James directed this question to each and every one of the members of 'the twelve tribes that are scattered about.' (Jas. 1:1)

The Wisdom from Above Among these Christians, who really had the needed wisdom and understanding to be a teacher of his fellow believers? This question calls for self-examination on the part of every man in the congregation. For one to be a teacher requires more than fine speaking ability or a clever mind. True wisdom and understanding are essential.

A genuinely wise person has a proper fear of

God and knows how to apply knowledge in a manner that will bring good results. (Prov. 9:10) One who possesses understanding is able to see into a matter, to get the sense of it and to discern the relationships of various aspects of a situation or circumstance and to grasp the full significance of what he is considering. He is a mature Christian, whose perceptive powers 'through use have been trained to distinguish both right and wrong.' (Heb. 5:14) His answers to questions also accurately reflect that wisdom. Especially should the teacher be wise and understanding as regards the Bible. This is the primary, all-essential wisdom to help oneself and others toward life. He must "get the sense" of the good news of the Kingdom 'with his heart.' (Matt. 13:15, 23)

Let him show out of his fine conduct his works

Just as faith is demonstrated by works, the possession of wisdom and understanding produces tangible evidence. This evidence takes the form of fine conduct. Since a profound, reverential fear of Jehovah is "the beginning of wisdom," the wise person is one who conducts himself in harmony with God's personality, ways and dealings. (Ps. 111:10) He obeys God's Word. A man cannot serve as a teacher unless he has fine conduct to recommend him.

with a mildness that belongs to wisdom

Mildness of temper is an essential feature of the kind of wisdom that should be displayed by any Christian, particularly by a man who qualifies to be a teacher of his fellow believers. In fact, the meek or mild ones are the only ones whom Jehovah will teach his way. (Ps. 25:9) A teacher must be gentle, calm and peaceful, not harsh, noisy and opinionated or arrogant. Neither should he be prone to make strong assertions without sound argument or proof to back them up, as did some professed teachers in the days of the apostles. (1 Tim. 1:6, 7) Though, unfortunately, some people may be impressed by statements loudly made with a tone of superiority, God is not. Strong volume will never compensate for a weak argument. (Compare Ecclesiastes 9:16, 17.)

A good example supporting the point James makes and demonstrating the need for teachers to exercise modesty, humility and love, is found in the first letter to the Corinthians, chapter 8. There the apostle Paul shows the real danger exists in a person's assuming that he knows something when in reality he does not have a full, rounded-out knowledge of the matter, the 'grasp' of the matter that is associated with true wisdom. The apostle shows that love is essential if a person is to use knowledge wisely.

Paul speaks to Christians living in an idolatrous world where meat was sanctified by being offered to an idol. Idol worshipers felt that this made the meat "holy," so that the eater would receive the approval of his idol god. Paul wrote: "Now concerning foods offered to idols: we know we all have knowledge." *An American Translation* renders the latter phrase as: "It is true, as you say, that we all have some knowledge on that matter." Phillips' *New Testament in Modern English* reads: "It is easy to think that we 'know' over problems like this." Paul then shows that such assumed knowledge could lead to immodest attitudes and an unwise course. He writes: "Knowledge ["Such knowledge," *Today's English Version;* "This 'knowledge,'" *The New English Bible*] puffs up, but love builds up. If anyone thinks he has acquired knowledge of something, he does not yet know it just as he ought to know it. Now concerning the eating of foods offered to idols, we know that an idol is nothing in the world, and that there is no God but one. Nevertheless, there is not this knowledge in all persons; but some, being ac-

14 But if you have bitter jealousy and contentious-ness in your hearts, do not be bragging and lying against the truth.

---

customed until now to the idol, eat food as some-thing sacrificed to an idol, and their conscience, being weak, is defiled." (1 Cor. 8:1, 2, 4, 7)

So a teacher might let his superior knowledge, or *supposed* knowledge, lead him into a trap. But modesty and humility will always be blessed and the humble person will be exalted. He will gain the confidence of those whom he teaches. Con-versely, the self-assured or arrogant teacher—one who is "always right," or who loves to make a display of his "knowledge," causing others to feel inferior—will create a "credibility gap" be-tween himself and those being taught.

14 But if you have bitter jealousy and conten-tiousness in your hearts

These words are evidently directed primarily to certain men who were very confident about being wise and able to teach their fellow believers. Such men should make an examination of their hearts. Did they harbor bitter jealousy? This bitter jealousy would include an inordinate desire to glorify themselves and their opinions, rather than to work sincerely for the good of their broth-ers, their upbuilding in faith and accurate knowl-edge. Jealousy and contentiousness are two of "the works of the flesh." (Gal. 5:19, 20, 26) These traits might manifest themselves (as the bitter water of the fountain previously mentioned) in a fanatical and stubborn zeal for their own views. At the same time such persons may loudly decry opinions differing from theirs, or fail to recognize and acknowledge that others possess wisdom and understanding equal to (or perhaps even superior to) their own.

All Christians, especially those aspiring to be teachers, should ask themselves whether they have any traces of jealousy or contentiousness in their hearts. Is theirs a spirit of quarreling and strife? Rather than being unbiased in a discussion of God's Word and the application of its principles, are they inclined to use means that cause contention in order to further their own ends? Such contentiousness would be the product of pride and selfish ambition—dangerous, deadly traits. These are the characteristics of the Devil. (1 Tim. 3:6; compare Proverbs 12:18.)

do not be bragging and lying against the truth

This counsel is directed to men who are bitterly jealous and contentious at heart. They should not try to elevate themselves to a position where these bad traits would become clearly manifest. By setting themselves up as teachers, they would be bragging about or boastfully calling attention to their assumed qualifications. Yet, Christian truth, which they professed to teach, condemns the bitter jealousy and contentiousness they have. Hence, a man who manifests a divisive spirit of rivalry and yet calls himself a Christian teacher is certainly misrepresenting or 'lying against the truth' of the "good news" that he claims to be teaching.

Furthermore, a man who exhibits such undesirable traits has *no basis* for bragging that he is qualified to teach his fellow believers. His doing so is a lie. The fact that he is self-seeking and quarrelsome at heart disqualifies him as a teacher of his brothers. Hence, by professing to be qualified, he would be lying against the truth, the actual state of affairs. Bible scholar F. J. A. Hort makes this perceptive comment: "The mere possession of truth is no security for true utterance of it: all utterance is so coloured by the moral and spiritual state of the speaker that truth issues

15 This is not the wisdom that comes down from above, but is the earthly, animal, demonic.

---

as falsehood from his lips in proportion as he himself is not in a right state: the correct language which he utters may carry a message of falsehood and evil in virtue of the bitterness and self-seeking which accompanies his speaking."

15 This is not the wisdom that comes down from above

The wisdom that self-seeking ambitious men claim to have does not come from God. The wisdom from God detests self-importance, bragging and power seeking, for Jehovah says: "This is what Jehovah has said: 'Let not the wise man brag about himself because of his wisdom, and let not the mighty man brag about himself because of his mightiness. Let not the rich man brag about himself because of his riches. But let the one bragging about himself brag about himself because of this very thing, the having of insight and the having of knowledge of me, that I am Jehovah, the One exercising loving-kindness, justice and righteousness in the earth; for in these things I do take delight,' is the utterance of Jehovah." (Jer. 9:23, 24) Men, teachers or whoever they are, may think they are serving God, but if they have a self-seeking spirit they are not genuinely his servants. Their works become worthless from God's standpoint. (1 Cor. 13:1) Divine wisdom stands in opposition to bitter jealousy and contentiousness.

but is the earthly, animal, demonic

The professed wisdom of such persons is of an earthly, not heavenly, nature. It is truly a certain *kind* of wisdom, one that is characteristic of earthlings alienated from God, who have no spirituality.

Worldlings expend their time and energies with a view to indulging their desires for pleasure. Or they may make efforts to attain prestige and possessions in this unstable, ever-changing system of things. (Phil. 3:19; Col. 3:2) Even in the Christian congregation such a spirit may manifest itself, just as it did among the congregations to which James wrote. Such fleshly wisdom may manifest great learning, tact, shrewdness, polish, skill and argumentation that appears on the surface to be logical and may be hard to refute. But we should keep in mind what Jesus said: "The sons of this system of things are wiser in a practical way toward their own generation than the sons of the light are." (Luke 16:8)

Contrastingly, the apostle Paul said of his teaching: "And so I, when I came to you, brothers, did not come with an extravagance of speech or of wisdom declaring the sacred secret of God to you. For I decided not to know anything among you except Jesus Christ, and him impaled. And I came to you in weakness and in fear and with much trembling; and my speech and what I preached were not with persuasive words of wisdom but with a demonstration of spirit and power, that your faith might be, not in men's wisdom, but in God's power." (1 Cor. 2:1-5)

The wisdom of a proud, quarrelsome man is also "animal," or, literally, "soulical," that is, it naturally comes from man's being a sentient creature, which is a soul. According to the Scriptures, both men and animals are souls. (Gen. 2:7; Num. 31:28; Rev. 16:3) Humans as sentient creatures (souls) are endowed with moral and intellectual capacity, but animals as sentient creatures are unreasoning. (2 Pet. 2:12; Jude 10) Hence, in being referred to as "animal," or soulical, this particular wisdom is shown to be unspiritual, the product of fleshly sensations, appetites and inclinations. It is even worse than that. It is demonic, for wicked spirits

16 For where jealousy and contentiousness are, there disorder and every vile thing are.
17 But the wisdom from above is first of all chaste, then peaceable, reasonable, ready to obey, full of mercy and good fruits, not making partial distinctions, not hypocritical.

---

manifest a like disposition. Hence, it is a fruitage of the Devil's spirit. The Bible reveals that Satan's downfall was, in fact, selfish pride and ambition. (1 Tim. 3:6)

16 For where jealousy and contentiousness are, there disorder and every vile thing are

Jealousy and contentiousness are destructive traits. They create an atmosphere wherein disorder and all manner of wickedness can flourish. Instability, insecurity, even chaos, take over, while happiness, security, peace and unity are destroyed. Love is absent. In the Christian congregation at Corinth, for example, jealousy and contentions were tearing the congregation apart into parties or factions. (1 Cor. 1:10-13; 3:3; 2 Cor. 12:20)

The 'vile things' could include rudeness, unfounded suspicions, hurtful gossip, slander, reviling, backbiting, enmities, vindictiveness, stubbornness, rebelliousness, hypocrisy, dissension, fights, favoritism, oppression and acts of violence. Those engaging in these things are in danger of actually 'annihilating one another' spiritually. (Gal. 5:15) But love "is a perfect bond of union." (Col. 3:14; 1 Cor. 13:4-7) How much happier the congregation is when its members follow Christ's command to love one another! Jealousy and contentiousness will then disappear.

17 But the wisdom from above is first of all chaste

The first quality of wisdom listed, chasteness or purity, is especially essential, its possession being necessary before any of the others can truly exist. The *heart* must be pure. The Christian having heavenly wisdom will reject evil without hesitation. Jesus, for example, instantly rejected Peter's well-meant proposal. He did not have to entertain or weigh the idea. (Matt. 16:21-23) The same was true in his reaction to Satan's temptations. (Matt. 4:1-10) Joseph saw the danger of the proposal made by Potiphar's wife. It would cause him to *sin against God,* and so he *immediately fled* when she tried to force herself on him. (Gen. 39:9, 12) A teacher needs this qualification preeminently, regardless of how many other good qualities he may have.

Heavenly wisdom is therefore the very opposite of the wisdom that is "earthly, animal, demonic." It is pure, undefiled, and does not provide the soil for all manner of uncleanness and wickedness, such as contentiousness, to grow. Its first or initial effect on individuals is to make them clean or pure in mind and heart. A good understanding of the scope of the word here translated "chaste" can be gained from 2 Corinthians 7:11.

then peaceable

Heavenly wisdom will make a person a promoter of peace. Not only will he avoid being aggressive or belligerent but he will also be a peacemaker, going out of his way to establish good relations between others. He will not engage in or approve of anything that disrupts peace. His words and example will encourage his fellowmen to be peaceable. (Rom. 14:19; Heb. 12:14) "Happy are the peaceable," said Jesus, "since they will be called 'sons of God.'" (Matt. 5:9)

reasonable

The wisdom from above makes a person reasonable, yielding, moderate or forbearing, not fanatical in his zeal. (Phil. 4:5; 1 Tim. 3:3; Titus 3:2)

Saul (Paul), directed by worldly wisdom, was misled by unreasoning fanaticism before he became a Christian. (Acts 9:1, 2; Gal. 1:13, 14) Unlike Saul, the reasonable person will not insist on his own way or on the letter of the law, but will look at a matter kindly, considerately and Scripturally, making effort to reason out the matter as Christ would.

The reasonable teacher will not be dogmatic. He will give thought to the state of advancement of those whom he is teaching, and to their circumstances. He will not put upon them more than they can bear at the time, and it may take a long time for them to see some things. Jesus said to his apostles who had been with him throughout his entire ministry: "I have many things yet to say to you, but you are not able to bear them at present." (John 16:12) A teacher recognizes that disciples, from the beginning of their Christian course, have many ideas, habits and customs that are not fully right. But they will change these habits when their hearts and consciences see clearly that they need to change. It is primarily God's spirit that has to induce them to make the change—not the teacher. If the one taught changes because *his teacher* says he must, instead of being motivated from the heart by the Scriptures, this will be of no value to him, because he is following, not God's Word and spirit, but a man.

Therefore, a good teacher will never lay down his own rules or regulations. He will let the Scriptures be the guide, with changes in their personality and ways being made by the learners as they come to a clear understanding. (Compare 1 Corinthians 9:19-23.)

ready to obey

Instead of stubbornness, heavenly wisdom promotes a spirit of cooperation, a willingness to respond to proper requests. A person with such qualities will yield to what the Scriptures say, not taking a position and holding to it, right or wrong. He will be quick to change when there is clear evidence that he has taken a wrong stand or has drawn erroneous conclusions. He makes the *Word of God* his guide and ultimate authority. (Rom. 6:17; 2 Tim. 4:2)

full of mercy and good fruits

The wisdom from above makes a man merciful, compassionate in his dealings with his fellow humans. He has pity for the afflicted and distressed and is eager and willing to do what he can to help them. If he is required to judge a matter involving some false step on the part of a member of the congregation, he has in mind *helping* the individual, if possible. (Jas. 5:19, 20; Jude 22, 23) Also, he does not mechanically apply rules, putting the individual in a certain "category," so that it is easy to apply the rule to him. Rather, he applies the Word of God with insight and with mercy, along with justice, taking into consideration all factors—the individual's background, his situation, the pressures on him, his desire to change, and so forth. He realizes that he himself is also of sinful flesh and could make a similar mistake. If he does not have this attitude, but feels superior or more righteous than another, he cannot be merciful, and he may find himself severely tempted, and may fall into sin also. (Compare Luke 18:9-14.) The apostle Paul says that we should help others who have made a misstep, and then he adds the warning: "Keep an eye on yourself, for fear you also may be tempted." (Gal. 6:1)

The "good fruits" include all actions that are in harmony with goodness, righteousness and truth. (Eph. 5:9) They are also expressions of active concern for others. (Compare 1 Timothy

5:10.) A teacher must be righteous, but even more than that, he should have goodness. The apostle Paul writes: "Hardly will anyone die for a righteous man; indeed, for the good man, perhaps, someone even dares to die." (Rom. 5:7) A man can be termed "righteous" if he fulfills his proper obligations, is just, impartial, honest, not guilty of wrongdoing or immorality; hence, he is known for integrity of conduct and uprightness. Paul's statement, however, implies a certain superiority in the "good" man. To be "good" the individual could not, of course, be unrighteous or unjust; yet other qualities distinguish him from the man primarily known for his righteousness. He is not merely concerned with doing what justice requires but goes beyond this, being motivated by wholesome consideration for others and the desire to benefit and help them.

not making partial distinctions

Earlier in his letter, James made clear that showing favoritism is a sin. (Jas. 2:1-9) The person who is guided by heavenly wisdom does not give preferential treatment to individuals based on their outward appearance, position, wealth or status in life, or their influence in the congregation. He strives to be impartial in his dealings with his fellowmen, particularly with his Christian brothers and sisters.*

not hypocritical

A hypocrite is one who pretends to be what he is not. His actions are out of harmony with his

---

* The Greek term for "not making partial distinctions" in some translations is rendered as "straightforward" and "without uncertainty." (*The New English Bible; Phillips' The New Testament in Modern English; Revised Standard Version*) The *Theological Dictionary of the New Testament* understands the term to mean "without doubts," "without wavering," "unshakeable." It is used in this way by some professed Christian writers of the early centuries. (See comments on James 2:4; 1:6-8.) Many translations, however, give renderings like that of the *New World Translation of the Holy Scriptures*.

18 Moreover, the fruit of righteousness has its seed sown under peaceful conditions for those who are making peace.

---

words. The Greek word metaphorically means to be stage-playing, acting. Actors often wore masks. Hypocrisy is one of the worst forms of sin, and can lead a person into all other sins, including sin against the holy spirit. The Pharisees are an example of this. (Matt. 23:23-28) Ananias and Sapphira are another. (Acts 5:1-10) These things serve as a warning to a person who aspires to be, or who is, a teacher. He has to be very careful, in every situation, to be open and not hypocritical. The apostle Paul specifically instructed Timothy as to the danger of hypocrisy in teaching. (1 Tim. 1:5-7) A hypocrite often is a "manipulator," for he is usually maneuvering to acquire some honor, status, position, advantage over others or material gain. (Compare 1 Thessalonians 1:5.) Ananias was evidently seeking position and prominence in the early Christian congregation, as some may do today.

The self-assertive, contentious person often plays the role of a hypocrite. He may put on a front of friendship in order to achieve his selfish ends. (Compare Jude 16.) He can be described as "playing politics," gaining adherents to his side for selfish purposes. However, the person who displays heavenly wisdom in his life does not wear a mask. In all his relations, he is upright, straightforward and trustworthy.

18 Moreover, the fruit of righteousness

James may here be speaking of righteousness as producing certain wholesome fruits in the lives of Christians. The prophet Isaiah speaks of the "work" and the "service" of righteousness: "In the orchard righteousness itself will dwell. And the work of the true righteousness must become peace; and the service of the true righteousness, quietness and security to time indefinite." (Isa. 32:16, 17) By following a course in harmony with true righteousness, Christians maintain a clean conscience before God and men, and enjoy contentment, satisfaction and a meaningful life.

Or, James may mean that righteousness is itself the desirable fruit. (Compare Hebrews 12:11.) This would be the righteousness that Jehovah God requires of his worshipers. When there is hatred, jealousy and lack of obedience to the Word of God, righteousness cannot be produced. Also, the good that comes from a life of righteousness will not be in evidence. The apostle Paul says: "The kingdom of God . . . means righteousness and peace and joy with holy spirit." (Rom. 14:17) To be righteous, a person must live in harmony with the "good news."

has its seed sown under peaceful conditions

For the seed of righteousness to grow, it must have the right conditions. A farmer does not sow seed in a field where a mob is rioting or where contentious persons are wrangling, but under calm, peaceful conditions. There must be peace, tranquillity, freedom from disturbance in the congregation for the seed of righteousness to develop and manifest itself and prosper spiritually, particularly for the members thereof to study God's Word and grow in depth of understanding and maturity.

The situation with the early Christian congregation shows how peaceful conditions facilitate spiritual growth. After the terrible persecution spearheaded by Saul of Tarsus quieted down, the record reads: "Then, indeed, the congregation throughout the whole of Judea and Galilee and Samaria entered into a period of peace, being built up; and as it walked in the fear of Jehovah and in the comfort of the holy spirit it kept on multiplying." (Acts 9:31) Especially *within* the congregation, if the fruit of righteousness is to be enjoyed, things that seriously disrupt peace must not be present. (Compare James 1:19-21.)

for those who are making peace

It is only the peacemakers who enjoy the "fruit of righteousness" that thrives under peaceful conditions. *The New Berkeley Version* renders James 3:18: "And the harvest, which righteousness yields to the peacemakers, comes from a sowing in peace." The peacemakers are persons who act peaceably and who strive to maintain and promote peace with and among their fellowmen. This peace is the opposite of jealousy and contentiousness. Such peace is based on an approved standing with Jehovah God.

Hence, of all people, teachers should be peacemakers who display the "wisdom from above." They should not be belligerent, quick to take up a quarrel, insisting that their personal opinions and standards be followed. (Gal. 5:25, 26) However, this does not mean that they should compromise Bible truth for the sake of peace. Nevertheless, a teacher can often keep peace by letting others maintain their own view, particularly in minor matters. At the same time he watches that the congregation has the correct understanding and is not contaminated or upset by wrong doctrine. (Compare Romans 14:1-4, 10; Titus 3:9-11.) He must recognize that "in a large house there are vessels not only of gold and silver but also of wood and earthenware, and some for an honorable purpose but others for a purpose lacking honor. If, therefore, anyone keeps clear of the latter ones, he will be a vessel for an honorable purpose, sanctified, useful to his owner, prepared for every good work." (2 Tim. 2:20, 21)

The teacher in the Christian congregation is

instructed to "turn down foolish and ignorant questionings, knowing they produce fights. But a slave of the Lord does not need to fight, but needs to be gentle toward all, qualified to teach, keeping himself restrained under evil, instructing with mildness those not favorably disposed; as perhaps God may give them repentance leading to an accurate knowledge of truth, and they may come back to their proper senses out from the snare of the Devil, seeing that they have been caught alive by him for the will of that one." (2 Tim. 2:23-26) Such a teacher will be a peace-maker.

QUESTIONS FOR STUDY

VERSE 1

Not many of you should become teachers, my brothers
  1 To whom is this portion of James' letter especially vital, and why?
  2 How do we know that James was not discouraging persons from proper teaching?
  3 Who only were assigned to be congregational teachers?
  4 What do the Scriptures show as to persons being notable in teaching activity?
  5 Why, then, does James say: "Not many of you should become teachers"?
  6 What would result if unqualified men were used as teachers in the congregation?
  7 What attitude toward teaching was prevalent among many in Israel?
  8 What example from the first century describes the results in the congregation when unqualified men are used as teachers?
  9 What factors concerning the responsibility of a teacher merit serious consideration?

knowing that we shall receive heavier judgment
  1 Why does a teacher receive heavier judgment, and therefore what would he constantly have to keep in mind?
  2 How did Jesus Christ show that our teaching will have a heavy bearing on the reward that we receive?

VERSE 2

For we all stumble many times

 1 Why do we all stumble many times?
 2 Why is this fact to be seriously noted by all who would be teachers?

If anyone does not stumble in word, this one is a perfect man

 1 How is it that one who does not stumble in word is a perfect man?
 2 Since no Christian is perfect, should he give up in trying to control his tongue? What should he do to this end?

able to bridle also his whole body

 1 What would be the result to a man who could bridle his tongue?

VERSE 3

If we put bridles in the mouths of horses for them to obey us, we manage also their whole body

 1 What does James' illustration here mean?

VERSE 4

Look! Even boats, although they are so big

 1 What makes this illustration a powerful one?

and are driven by hard winds, are steered by a very small rudder to where the inclination of the man at the helm wishes

 1 What factors make the control of a ship by its rudder an amazing thing?

VERSE 5

So, too, the tongue is a little member

 1 How are the illustrations of a horse and a ship comparable with the human body?
 2 Who need to give *special* attention to the counsel James is giving in this chapter?

and yet makes great brags

 1 Can the tongue indeed exert much power?
 2 What do the Scriptures say about those who use the tongue for boasting?

Look! How little a fire it takes to set so great a woodland on fire

 1 Why does James now use the illustration of a fire?

VERSE 6

Well, the tongue is a fire

 1 In accord with what motivates it, how is the tongue "fiery"?

The tongue is constituted a world of unrighteousness among our members
1 How is the tongue "a world of unrighteousness"?
2 What are some of the ways in which the tongue has been wrongly used?

for it spots up all the body
1 In what way does the tongue spot up a person's entire body?

and sets the wheel of natural life aflame
1 What is "the wheel of natural life"?
2 How does the tongue set this wheel aflame?

and it is set aflame by Gehenna
1 How did the word "Gehenna" come to have the significance it has in Bible usage?
2 How did Jesus confirm the above-mentioned understanding of the meaning of "Gehenna"?
3 Explain this expression, "it is set aflame by Gehenna."
4 His tongue being "set aflame by Gehenna," in what great danger also is the person with such a tongue, as shown by Jesus?

VERSE 7

For every species of wild beast
1 What does James mean by "every species"?
2 On what Scriptural basis has man been able to tame wild beasts?

as well as bird
1 Show that birds are included in the things man has tamed.

and creeping thing
1 How does the Bible agree with our common knowledge that creeping things have been tamed?

and sea creature
1 To what extent has man been able to tame some of the sea creatures?

is to be tamed and has been tamed by humankind
1 How widespread does man's ability seem to extend as to taming animals?

VERSE 8

But the tongue, not one of mankind can get it tamed
1 How hard a job is it to tame the tongue?

An unruly injurious thing, it is full of death-dealing poison
1 How bad is the untamed tongue?

2 How did the tongue come to be more untamable than animals are?

3 How is the tongue "full of death-dealing poison"?

4 What examples show us the widespread bad effect of such a tongue?

VERSE 9

With it we bless Jehovah, even the Father, and yet with it we curse men who have come into existence "in the likeness of God"

1 For whom is Jehovah "the Father," and how?

2 What force does this give to James' counsel?

3 How was man made in God's likeness, and how does this emphasize the point that James is making?

4 What does it mean to "curse" someone?

5 Under what circumstances was proper cursing done?

6 Why is it so bad to curse other persons?

7 Why can a tongue that is cursing men not be blessing God?

8 If we use our tongue wisely almost all the time, can we feel perfectly safe that we will not slip and misuse it on some occasion?

VERSE 10

Out of the same mouth come forth blessing and cursing

1 How is it contradictory for both blessing and cursing to come forth from the same mouth?

It is not proper, my brothers, for these things to go on occurring this way

1 Should we utter curses at all, even in our own hearts?

2 How would such double use of the tongue reveal a corrupt heart?

VERSE 11

A fountain does not cause the sweet and the bitter to bubble out of the same opening, does it?

1 What is the point James is making by this statement?

2 Why is it that only in humankind do we find something so unnatural?

VERSE 12

My brothers, a fig tree cannot produce olives or a vine figs, can it?

1 What law of God prevents this from taking place?

2 What is the difference between this illustration and the one just discussed?

3 What is the point of this illustration?

Neither can salt water produce sweet water

1 How is this illustration in one respect a contrast to the previous one?

2 What is revealed about the person whose tongue brings forth speech that is good and refreshing and also that which is distasteful, bad?

3 How did Jesus illustrate the great danger confronting the one whose tongue does not agree with what he professes to be as a person?

VERSE 13

Who is wise and understanding among you?

1 This question calls for self-examination along what lines?

2 Describe the truly wise person.

3 In respect to what, above all things, should the teacher be wise and understanding?

Let him show out of his fine conduct his works

1 What is foremost in revealing that a person has wisdom?

2 How is the fear of Jehovah the beginning of wisdom?

with a mildness that belongs to wisdom

1 More than mere knowledge, what qualifies a teacher, and why?

2 What does the apostle Paul say that knowledge may do for a person?

3 How does the apostle show that one who relies on assumed knowledge may act unwisely?

4 Describe the difference in effects of the teacher who takes pride in his knowledge and of the modest, humble one.

VERSE 14

But if you have bitter jealousy and contentiousness in your hearts

1 What would bitter jealousy include?

2 What would be the action and attitude of such persons?

3 What questions should all, especially those who desire to be teachers, ask themselves?

4 What great danger lies in a jealous and contentious spirit?

do not be bragging and lying against the truth

1 How could a person, especially one who assumes to be a teacher, 'brag and lie against the truth'?
2 Why, even though a teacher has a very good knowledge, would he be disqualified if he has a jealous disposition or attitude?

VERSE 15

This is not the wisdom that comes down from above
1 Show, from God's Word, that those seeking importance and power do not have the wisdom from above.

but is the earthly, animal, demonic
1 How is the wisdom that has the spirit of jealousy and contentiousness properly called "earthly"?
2 How does such wisdom contrast with the wisdom of the true representatives of Christ?
3 How is the wisdom of a proud man "animal" or "soulical"? How is it "demonic"?

VERSE 16

For where jealousy and contentiousness are, there disorder and every vile thing are
1 What happens in a congregation where these bad traits exist, as illustrated in the congregation in Corinth?
2 What are some of the "vile" things that jealousy and contentiousness bring into the Christian congregation?

VERSE 17

But the wisdom from above is first of all chaste
1 Why is chasteness preeminently necessary, and why should teachers, especially, seek this quality?
2 How is heavenly wisdom the very opposite of the wisdom that is "earthly, animal, demonic"?
3 How does 2 Corinthians 7:11 show how chasteness views wrongdoing?

then peaceable
1 In what ways will heavenly wisdom manifest itself as peaceable?

reasonable
1 How does reasonableness prevent a Christian from becoming fanatical?
2 How is a true teacher reasonable with those whom he is teaching?
3 Why is it not true wisdom to get a person to change his ways before he sees, in his heart, the necessity to do so?

ready to obey

1 How does a person show himself "ready to obey"?

full of mercy and good fruits

1 What does mercy prompt the Christian to do when he is called upon to correct or reprove a brother for some false step or some wrong into which he has fallen?

2 If he feels a superior attitude, as if to say, 'I would never do such a thing as this brother did,' in what danger is he placing himself?

3 What are the "good fruits" that the wisdom from above produces?

4 "Goodness" being one of the fruits of the spirit, how can it be described or illustrated?

not making partial distinctions

1 What is included in "not making partial distinctions"?

not hypocritical

1 Why is hypocrisy so dangerous and damaging?

2 Give an example showing how hypocrisy acts.

3 What is the difference between the one who displays heavenly wisdom and the hypocrite?

VERSE 18

Moreover, the fruit of righteousness

1 In what way may James here be speaking of "the fruit of righteousness"?

2 In what other way may this expression be understood?

has its seed sown under peaceful conditions

1 Why must conditions in a congregation be peaceful for seed to be successfully sown?

2 What example do we have showing that peaceableness is essential to growth in depth of understanding and maturity?

for those who are making peace

1 Who enjoy the fruit of righteousness, the seed of which is sown in peace?

2 How can a good teacher keep peace without compromising on the truth?

3 Why is a teacher to turn down foolish questionings that really do not have to do with faith, and that produce fights?

CHAPTER 4

1 From what source are there wars and from what source are there fights among you? Are they not from this source, namely, from your cravings for sensual pleasure that carry on a conflict in your members?

---

1 From what source are there wars and from what source are there fights among you?

As is evident from what the disciple James wrote earlier, among Christians there were certain serious problems that would not contribute to unity. Favoritism was being shown to the rich. Love was not being allowed to have its full expression, as some were wrongly judging their brothers and failing to respond to the needs of their fellow Christians. A spirit of strife existed. Jealousy and contentiousness had gained a foothold in the congregation.

Wrong Desires Destructive

As a result, peace was disrupted. Hence, the question logically presented itself, What is the source of this warring and fighting among Christians? (Compare Galatians 5:15.)

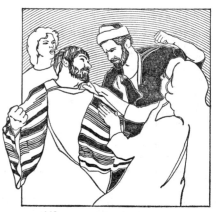

Are they not

from this source, namely, from your cravings for sensual pleasure that carry on a conflict in your members?

The source of the problem was wrong cravings or desires in the body members of these Christians. There was a longing for and a consequent satisfying of sensual gratification in the fallen flesh. The Greek word translated "carry on a conflict" literally means "doing military service." (*Kingdom Interlinear Translation*) These cravings, the result of inherited sin, were like an invading army that was campaigning in each Christian, using as its encampment his whole body, thereby causing fights and larger conflicts—in effect, wars—in the congregation. The fleshly craving for importance, possessions and the like was exerting strong influence on the individual Christian and affecting his relationship with his fellow Christians. Also, since the conscience would be indicating that such fulfillment of desire for pleasures was selfish, a spiritual turmoil ensued within each Christian.

In this connection, we may note that the Christian apostle Paul sensed keenly the conflict that sin in his body members brought about inside him. To his fellow believers in Rome, he wrote: "When I wish to do what is right, what is bad is present with me. I really delight in the law of God according to the man I am within, but I behold in my members another law warring against the law of my mind and leading me captive to sin's law that is in my members." (Rom. 7:21-23) The apostle Peter similarly speaks of "fleshly desires, which are the very ones that carry on a conflict against the soul." (1 Pet. 2:11) Paul also said of himself: "I pummel my body and lead it as a slave, that, after I have preached to others, I myself should not become disapproved somehow." (1 Cor. 9:27)

Whenever wrong fleshly cravings are allowed by an individual to win out in this inner struggle,

2 You desire, and yet you do not have. You go on murdering and coveting, and yet you are not able to obtain. You go on fighting and waging war. You do not have because of your not asking.

---

peace may be disrupted in the congregation. Justice, love and righteousness, with mercy, on the other hand, are never the cause of any conflict. But the person who is ruled by a wrong craving, such as ambition, desire for greater control or influence, puts himself ahead of others and may become vindictive and vengeful when others seem to stand in the way of his achieving his goals. He will have a warring spirit.

2 You desire, and yet you do not have

Since there was no punctuation in the original manuscripts, this verse (2) has been rendered differently by various translators.* (The *New World Translation,* however, has the support of many other modern-language translations.) James does not specify just what the individual might desire. He undoubtedly meant that the things desired were to gratify a craving for pleasure, or were for things of an immoral or materialistic nature, or, perhaps, for power, position, the plaudits of others, and so forth. This is the opinion of F. J. A. Hort, the coproducer of the punctuated Greek text of the Christian Greek Scriptures, who said that in this context the word here translated "desire" expresses envy of position or rank or fame, sordid and bitter personal ambition.† The thing desired could well be something to which the

---

* The *Revised Standard Version* renders verse 2 as describing cause and effect in the first three clauses. It reads as a parallelism: "You desire and do not have; so you kill. And you covet and cannot obtain; so you fight and wage war. You do not have, because you do not ask." However, the footnote of this verse agrees with the *New World Translation* in its punctuation. See also the comment on James 4:2 in *The International Critical Commentary,* by Driver, Plummer and Briggs.

† *The Epistle of St. James,* a Greek text with commentary.

person was not entitled or that simply was not within his reach. Though he could not obtain the object of his craving through honest means, he did not put it out of his mind. He continued desiring what he did not have.

You go on murdering and coveting

The desire for what could not be honorably obtained—as, for example, by work or by honest, well-motivated effort—was allowed to grow. We may note that the apostate "man of lawlessness" is shown by Paul to be motivated by a strong desire for adulation and power. (2 Thess. 2:3, 4) The covetousness in the Christians to whom James wrote had developed to the point of its giving rise to a hateful, murderous spirit.

Lack of love for their brothers in the household of faith was being exhibited by certain Christians, who, on seeing their fellow Christians in need, refused to give help. They greedily clung to what they had while seeking things to which they were not entitled or that were beyond their reach through honest means. (Compare James 2:14-16; 1 John 2:15-17; 3:15, 17.)

World history, and even the history of the ancient nation of Israel, shows how wrong desire can result in murder. Note with what swiftness it entered the human race and led to the murder of Abel by his brother Cain, the firstborn son of Adam and Eve. Also, consider how coveting on the part of King Ahab of Israel caused him to allow the murder of Naboth at the instance of his wife Jezebel. (Gen. 4:8; 1 Ki. 21:2-16)

and yet you are not able to obtain

They could not obtain the things desired because the desires were wrong, and such things had no blessing from God. They could not be obtained by fair and honest means, especially in the congregation of God.

3 You do ask, and yet you do not receive, because you are asking for a wrong purpose, that you may expend it upon your cravings for sensual pleasure.

You go on fighting and waging war

Because their covetousness and their vicious, hateful ways left their desires unfulfilled, they kept on fighting and warring in an effort to attain their goals. Such things are very evident in the world. But, to a limited extent, the same spirit and the same actions had actually developed in the congregations, and this can be the case today if heavenly wisdom, unity and peace are not sought by the congregation's members, including those taking the lead.

You do not have because of your not asking

On account of conducting themselves in a hateful manner, some of the persons addressed by James simply could not approach Jehovah God in a pure way. (Compare Lamentations 3:44.) They knew that God would not grant these desires, but they did not want to change and pray for the proper things according to his will. (1 John 5:14) If they had asked for what they really needed and for the things that would help them and others spiritually, God would have granted them. And whether they received the things asked for or not, they could be sure that God would withhold things only because it was best that they did not have them. He would supply other things that would serve much better for their welfare.

3 You do ask, and yet you do not receive

When they did ask, their requests were not rightly motivated. Because these requests did not involve genuine needs and were not in harmony with God's will, they were not answered. The apostle John wrote: "Whatever we ask we receive from him, because we are observing his commandments and are doing the things that are pleasing in his eyes." (1 John 3:22) Also, Jehovah is the One who opens his hand and satisfies the desire of every living thing. (Ps. 145:16) However, those whom James had in mind did not receive anything because their object in asking was wrong.

because you are asking for a wrong purpose, that you may expend it upon your cravings for sensual pleasure

Here James reveals that, whatever they were desiring, it was in each case something that the individual thought would bring him pleasure, without regard to its rightness or wrongness and with little or no consideration for others, for helping or upbuilding them. They did not have the right reason for their request. Being wrongly motivated and not considering Jehovah's will in the matter, they did not pray with a view to their being in a better position to help others, especially the poor and the afflicted. Instead, they asked God to help them to indulge their sensual pleasures. They wanted a life of self-gratification and ease. In God's eyes it was as if they were not praying at all. The way that God views such prayers is described at Proverbs 28:9: "He that is turning his ear away from hearing the law—even his prayer is something detestable." (Compare Isaiah 1:15; 1 Peter 3:12.) Persons with such attitudes could fall into the sad state of those mentioned by Peter: "They consider luxurious living in the daytime a pleasure. They are spots and blemishes, indulging with unrestrained delight in their deceptive teachings while feasting together with you." (2 Pet. 2:13)

On this point, *The International Critical Commentary* makes a pertinent observation: "The only sure source from which men can always re-

4 Adulteresses, do you not know that the friendship with the world is enmity with God? Whoever, therefore, wants to be a friend of the world is constituting himself an enemy of God.

---

ceive is God. By choosing pleasure as their aim, men cut themselves off from this source, for they do not ask God for gratifications such as these, or, if they do, only find that their prayers, aiming at their own pleasures and not at his service, are unacceptable, and that they ought not to have offered them.

"James's principle is: Make the service of God your supreme end, and then your desires will be such as God can fulfil in answer to your prayer (cf. Mt. 6³¹⁻³³). Then there will be none of the present strife. Pleasures war, and cause war. Desire for pleasure, when made the controlling end, leads to violence, for longings then arise which can only be satisfied by the use of violence, since God, from whom alone come good things (1¹⁷), will not satisfy them."

4 Adulteresses

The Christian congregation is viewed in Scripture as a bride and must, therefore, preserve virgin purity or chastity. (2 Cor. 11:2) Any unfaithfulness to the Christ also constitutes disloyalty to his Father. Even in pre-Christian times, Jehovah God regarded the unfaithfulness of the Israelites as adultery. Israel, for example, was guilty of prostitution when the people became involved in idolatry or when, instead of looking to Jehovah, they began looking to foreign nations for protection. (Ezek. 16:15-19, 25-45) Because they had turned away from God, Jesus called his generation an "adulterous" one. (Matt. 12:39) Hence, in addressing certain Chris-

Friendship with the World

tians as adulteresses, the disciple James was showing that they were no longer pure from the standpoint of Jehovah God and Jesus Christ.

**do you not know that the friendship with the
world is enmity with God?**

James uses the question form for emphasis and
to prick the consciences of his brothers, who knew
or certainly should have known this fact. By
friendship with the world, James refers to the
community or people called "the world," as dis-
tinguished from God's people, Christians. Such
friendship constitutes spiritual adultery. This
world caters to fleshly desires, as described by
the apostle John, at 1 John 2:16: "Everything in
the world—the desire of the flesh and the desire
of the eyes and the showy display of one's means
of life—does not originate with the Father, but
originates with the world." This friendship manifests itself in a person's being like the world in
attitude, goals, methods and action.

The Christian who fails to center his life on
his service to God and makes the pursuit of material possessions, position or the like his main
objective in life is acting just as the world does.
He gives no evidence that he has his sight on the
things unseen or that he is working diligently to
store up treasures in heaven, that is, making a
record of fine works with the Most High. (Matt.
6:20; 2 Cor. 4:18)

**Whoever, therefore, wants to be a friend of the
world is constituting himself an enemy of God**

Christians are to be no part of the world in
attitude, speech or ways. The Son of God said
respecting his faithful apostles: "The world has
hated them, because they are no part of the
world, just as I am no part of the world." (John
17:14) Therefore, the Christian who desires and

5 Or does it seem to you that the scripture says to no purpose: "It is with a tendency to envy that the spirit which has taken up residence within us keeps longing"?

---

seeks the world's friendship must change in such a way that he will no longer be an object of its hatred. He must make himself acceptable to worldlings who have no regard for spiritual things. This requires a compromise on his part, a lack of firm, unwavering loyalty to Christ. He must adopt many of the very viewpoints, words and often the actions and methods that are contrary to what God expects of his servants. If a Christian voluntarily selects worldly companions as his intimate or regular associates, he is "testing" God and 'inciting him to jealousy.' (1 Cor. 10:22; 2 Cor. 6:14)

Since love for God is displayed by obedience, all who seek the world's friendship are really showing hatred for the Most High, making themselves his enemies. We cannot serve two masters. (Matt. 6:24) The Christians whom James was addressing had made themselves enemies of God by yielding to covetousness and warring.

5 Or does it seem to you that the scripture says to no purpose

This phrase introduces a point about the tendency to envy. There is no specific text in the Hebrew Scriptures that fits the words quoted or stated by the disciple James. Evidently he had in mind the *teaching,* or sense, sentiment, of the Hebrew Scriptures as a whole, rather than a specific quotation. Jesus emphasized getting the *sense* of what God has to say. (Matt. 13:19, 23) And the inspired Christian writers often paraphrased texts from the Hebrew Scriptures, giving the sense or the application in principle where there was a similar or parallel circumstance.

(Compare Acts 1:20 with Psalm 69:25 and 109:8; John 19:36 with Exodus 12:46.)

"It is with a tendency to envy that the spirit which has taken up residence within us keeps longing"

This agrees with what Jehovah God declared right after the global deluge: "Never again shall I call down evil upon the ground on man's account, because the inclination of the heart of man is bad from his youth up." (Gen. 8:21) Part of that bad inclination is the tendency to envy. That envy does contribute to strife and fights is well illustrated in the case of Dathan and Abiram. Stirred by envy, they made a vicious verbal attack on Moses and Aaron. (Num. 16:1-3; Ps. 106:16, 17) The warring that James described earlier stemmed from the same envious spirit. It was certainly not without purpose, emptily or in vain that the Hebrew Scriptures point to sinful man's tendency to envy.

This tendency can be readily discerned among humans today, confirming what the Bible says. Envy is rooted in selfishness. The envious person may resort to fraud, robbery or other dishonest means to get what others have. (Prov. 21:10) Or, he may downgrade the one whom he envies, minimizing the accomplishments of that one by undue criticism or by calling into question his abilities and motives. The tendency to envy keeps pushing sinful humans in the wrong direction. From the surface appearance, a man may work very hard and efficiently. However, envy may be prompting him to attain what others have and even to surpass them. This produces rivalry. (Eccl. 4:4)

The word translated "longing" has the thought of "yearning" or "yearning over." (Compare the use of the word in 2 Corinthians 9:14; Philippians 1:8.) At 1 Peter 2:2 the apostle uses it with

6 However, the undeserved kindness which he gives is greater. Hence it says: "God opposes the haughty ones, but he gives undeserved kindness to the humble ones."

---

reference to the longing of those like "newborn infants" for the milk of God's Word.*

6 However, the undeserved kindness which he gives is greater

Though the selfish tendency to envy exerts a tremendous pressure on sinful humans, another force can counteract this. That force is supplied by the undeserved kindness coming from God. The help that comes through God's spirit is certainly an expression of divine undeserved kindness. This help enables a person to keep bad inclinations from getting out of control. Hence, the undeserved kindness that God gives is far greater or more powerful than the tendency to envy. The apostle

* Greek scholars generally view James 4:5 as a very difficult text to translate. Translations with renderings similar to that of the *New World Translation* include the *Authorized Version; Douay; Lamsa; Syriac New Testament.* Other translations differ and the reason for this is explained in *A Textual Commentary on the Greek New Testament.* Regarding the verb for "residing" or "dwelling" used at James 4:5, this commentary points out that there are two verbal forms that sound very much alike but differ in one letter. One form is causative, the other intransitive. As the commentary states: "*katókisen* is causative ('The spirit which he [God] has made to dwell in us'), whereas *katókēsen* is intransitive ('the spirit [or, Spirit] which dwells in us')." The causative form is found in the most ancient complete manuscripts.

Some translators understand the "spirit" referred to as meaning God's holy spirit and the sense of the text to be that 'the spirit which God placed in us yearns toward us jealously.' (The usual sense of the Greek term *phthónos* is envy, ill will or malice; it is, however, at times used in Greek writings to mean jealousy or indignation.) *The Jerusalem Bible* reads: "The spirit which he sent to live in us wants us for himself alone." (See also the *New Berkeley Version; Weymouth; The New Testament in Basic English, Knox.*) Others understand the "yearning" or "longing" to be done by God in the sense of his desiring his servants' whole-souled love, with no room for the world's rivalry. Thus the *Revised Standard Version* reads: "He yearns jealously over the spirit which he has made to dwell in us." (See also *Moffatt; An American Translation; The Translator's New Testament.*)

7 Subject yourselves, therefore, to God; but oppose the Devil, and he will flee from you.

Paul wrote: "Keep walking by spirit and you will carry out no fleshly desire at all." (Gal. 5:16)

It is also true that God resists the haughty ones who seek success and prominence or friendship with the world, but he gives undeserved kindness to those who humbly look to him, following the direction in which his spirit inclines them. The strength God gives is far greater than the forces working against the Christian. And while God rigorously requires his people to give him exclusive devotion, he richly pours out his undeserved kindness that is more than enough to enable them to conquer the world with its many appeals to turn to it and become its friends.

Hence it says

Proving that the undeserved kindness of God is greater, the scripture says:

God opposes the haughty ones, but he gives undeserved kindness to the humble ones

This is a quotation from the *Septuagint* rendering of Proverbs 3:34. Those who are humble at heart greatly desire and persistently pray for Jehovah's help and guidance. They obey him in order to gain his friendship. That is why, by God's undeserved kindness, which he showers upon them abundantly, they are able to gain the mastery over their own sinful tendencies and over the pressures the world brings upon them. Though they are imperfect sinners, Jehovah is pleased to come to their aid, but in no way will he favor the arrogant or "haughty." (1 Pet. 5:5)

7 Subject yourselves, therefore, to God

James describes how Christians can have the

undeserved kindness mentioned in verse 6. They must yield, be submissive to God in everything, not only in what he commands,

Change of Heart Needed

but in all the things he provides or allows to come upon them, knowing that he is working out all things for their ultimate good. We are assured of this at Romans 8:28. We must make a determined stand to keep on submitting fully. Peter says: "Humble yourselves, therefore, under the mighty hand of God, that he may exalt you in due time." (1 Pet. 5:6)

but oppose the Devil

In verse 6, according to the Greek word, God "is ranging himself against" the haughty; the Christian should 'range himself' or "stand against" the Devil. (*Kingdom Interlinear Translation;* compare Ephesians 6:10-17.) The world is in harmony with the Devil, because he is its "god." (2 Cor. 4:4) He appeals to traits that the world exalts, such as independence, pride, selfishness, love of position, prominence, fame, materialistic gain, and so forth. (Compare Ephesians 4:26, 27.) He also often employs agencies and organizations of the world in his fight.

and he will flee from you

The Devil is defeated and has to abandon his attack because, by submission to God, Christians have the help of Jesus Christ, who conquered the world. (John 16:33) The Devil fled when Jesus, by proper use of the Scriptures, resisted his attack. (Matt. 4:11) Later Jesus said: "The ruler of the world is coming. And he has no hold on me," and "now there is a judging of this world; now the ruler of this world will be cast out." (John 14:30; 12:31) Christians have the comfort of knowing that Jesus fights for them, re-

8 Draw close to God, and he will draw close to you. Cleanse your hands, you sinners, and purify your hearts, you indecisive ones.

---

straining the evil agencies of the world to the extent necessary, and that nothing can harm them in any lasting sense. The Scriptures say: "Indeed, who is the man that will harm you if you become zealous for what is good?" (1 Pet. 3:13) The psalmist also assures us full protection. (Ps. 91: 9-12)

8 Draw close to God, and he will draw close to you

By prayer, repentance, obedience and devotion to God, Christians draw close to him, and he is always near so as to respond to the humble ones. "Jehovah is with you as long as you prove to be with him; and if you search for him, he will let himself be found by you, but if you leave him he will leave you." (2 Chron. 15:2)

Cleanse your hands, you sinners, and purify your hearts, you indecisive ones

Those to whom James wrote were guilty of "wars" and 'murders' among themselves. Not that any had actually committed literal murder, but they were guilty of murderous hate, backbiting, slander, and so forth. In urging them to 'cleanse their hands,' James may have had in mind Isaiah 1:15, 16, addressed to unfaithful Israel: "With bloodshed your very hands have become filled. Wash yourselves; make yourselves clean; remove the badness of your dealings from in front of my eyes; cease to do bad."

The Christians to whom James wrote were addressed as "sinners," for they needed to repent and to change from a bad course. "Hands" have to do with deeds, for most works are performed with the hands. Sinful deeds taint the hands. The heart represents the chief seat of motivation and will, prompting our actions. The heart, from which wicked thoughts flow, must be made clean in order for good deeds to be produced. (Matt. 15:19) Not merely the outward *deeds* but also the inward *person* must be cleansed. No one can do this without the purifying power of the holy spirit.

James' readers included many who were double-minded, doubting, wavering persons. Their hearts were not steady. They were swaying back and forth. They had allowed their bad inclinations to lead them into a dangerous state. They needed to remove the disturbing things from their hearts, so that they would be all one way, pure and undivided. They were vacillating between friendship with God and friendship with the world, which was, figuratively, adultery.

The fact that those Christians in the days of the apostles had fallen into such a bad spiritual condition should make us think seriously, for, just as they undoubtedly felt that they were faithfully serving Christ but did not see their spiritually destitute state, the same thing can happen to us. Look at the situation of the congregation in Laodicea, to which Christ sent a special corrective warning message: "Because you say: 'I am rich and have acquired riches and do not need anything at all,' but you do not know you are miser-

9 Give way to misery and mourn and weep. Let your laughter be turned into mourning, and your joy into dejection.

---

able and pitiable and poor and blind and naked, I advise you to buy from me gold refined by fire that you may become rich, and white outer garments that you may become dressed and that the shame of your nakedness may not become manifested, and eyesalve to rub in your eyes that you may see." (Rev. 3:17, 18)

A Christian's own inherent sinfulness and the influence of the world tend to pull him in a direction away from the truth even before he is aware of it. (Compare Romans 7:18, 19.) For this reason we must exercise unceasing vigilance.

9 Give way to misery and mourn and weep

James is not counseling Christians to be joyless, constantly presenting a sad outlook and a long face. The Bible commands Jehovah's people to rejoice "in every undertaking" as they apply Bible principles in their everyday lives and as they give material and spiritual help to others, even when they are persecuted for Christ's sake. (Deut. 12:7; Phil. 4:4; Luke 6:22, 23) But when we do wrong our conscience should make us uncomfortable. When David had done wrong his heart "beat" him, and he was miserable, recognizing that his sin was primarily against God; and he made every effort to regain the favor of God. (2 Sam. 24:10; Pss. 38:1-7; 51:1-4)

Let your laughter be turned into mourning, and your joy into dejection

The apostle Paul wrote to Christians who had been reproved because of sinfulness that was in their midst: "Sadness in a godly way makes for repentance to salvation that is not to be regretted;

10 Humble yourselves in the eyes of Jehovah, and he will exalt you.

---

but the sadness of the world produces death. For, look! this very thing, your being saddened in a godly way, what a great earnestness it produced in you." (2 Cor. 7:10, 11) "Better is vexation than laughter, for by the crossness of the face the heart becomes better," says Ecclesiastes 7:3. The right kind of sadness results in beneficial discipline. (Heb. 12:11) Even though the apostle Paul had great joy and success in his work, the constant conflict between his renewed Christian mind and his inherently sinful body made him exclaim: "Miserable man that I am!" (Rom. 7:24) The realization of this sad fact and his working to get better control of the sinful tendencies of his imperfect flesh helped Paul to be a better Christian.

James admonishes those who were trying to be friends of the world and at the same time were feeling that they were serving God to give sober thought to their true position, to leave the carefree, lighthearted attitude into which they had been drawn and to be dejected and aware of their spiritual need, mourning over the bad situation in which they found themselves. (Matt. 5:3, 4) Jesus commended the tax collector who went to the temple to pray, and who, "standing at a distance was not willing even to raise his eyes heavenward, but kept beating his breast, saying, 'O God, be gracious to me a sinner.'" (Luke 18:13; compare Luke 6:25.)

10 Humble yourselves in the eyes of Jehovah, and he will exalt you

Jesus Christ said: "Whoever exalts himself will be humbled, and whoever humbles himself will be exalted." (Matt. 23:12) Since all sins committed

11 Quit speaking against one another, brothers. He who speaks against a brother or judges his brother speaks against law and judges law. Now if you judge law, you are, not a doer of law, but a judge.

---

are against God, we must humble ourselves *in his sight*. The prodigal son said to his father: "Father, I have sinned against heaven and against you. I am no longer worthy of being called your son. Make me as one of your hired men." Seeing this condition of heart in his son, the father received him back, giving him honor and a feast to celebrate his return. (Luke 15:21-24) Similarly, the tax collector went to his home with a better standing before God than the self-exalted Pharisee, according to the rule stated a little differently by the inspired writer Luke: "Everyone that exalts himself will be humiliated, but he that humbles himself will be exalted." (Luke 18:14; 14:11)

King David said: "The sacrifices to God are a broken spirit; a heart broken and crushed, O God, you will not despise." (Ps. 51:17) No sacrifice will avail us anything with God unless we acknowledge our sins, and any hardness of heart is softened, and any haughty or lighthearted attitude toward our sinful condition is removed. When we realize that we ourselves are nothing and when God is everything to us, then we can expect his favor. We will have a feeling of exaltation now, the heavy burden our sin has brought on our conscience being lifted. God will renew our spirit, and we will have freeness of speech to speak to others about his loving-kindness and his purposes. (Ps. 51:10, 12, 13)

11 Quit speaking against one another, brothers

In the preceding portion of his letter James dealt with the problem of haughtiness and a lack

of humility. This may have been at the root of
the problem he now takes up, namely, that of
speaking against one's brother.

**Do Not Judge
One Another**

(Compare Psalm 101:5.) Since
James has already dealt with
the matter of 'cursing' one's
brother, something often born
of the heat of anger or bitter hatred, this section
must deal with another facet of a wrong attitude
toward one's brother. It is a strongly critical attitude that now comes in for attention.

By saying "brothers," James emphasizes the
greatness of the wrong. Often it is the desire to
exalt himself that motivates a person to speak
against another, downgrading that one and making him appear inferior. The psalmist said of
such a one: "You sit and speak against your own
brother, against the son of your mother you give
away a fault." (Ps. 50:20) Also, a self-righteous
attitude can make a person inclined to be critical
of others and their actions or ways, even to the

point of incriminating them. (John 9:13-16, 28, 34) Whatever the motive, such derogatory speech has no rightful place among brothers in the household of faith. (Compare Leviticus 19:16; Proverbs 3:29, 30.) Because of inherited sinfulness, the human tendency in this direction is common and so James' counsel is of great value.

He who speaks against a brother or judges his brother

Clearly, it is not wrong to speak against acts or conduct that are condemned in God's Word. Christian elders in particular are called upon to reprove, even with severity, those engaging in sinful conduct; and all in the congregation are responsible to manifest their disapproval of such. (1 Cor. 5:1-5, 9-13; Eph. 5:3, 11; 2 Thess. 3:6, 11-15; 1 Tim. 5:20; 2 Tim. 4:2; Titus 1:9-13) But in all cases, the actions or conduct dealt with are such as are shown in God's Word itself to be sinful. *His* word, *his* law, thus provided the reproof and did the judging. Christian elders faithfully conveyed or expressed this divine reproof and God's declared judgment. James himself gives such reproof in his letter, showing forcefully the wrongness of worship that is carried on in word but not in deed, of partiality, of dissension and of fighting among brothers. Wherein, then, lies the difference between this and the course that James now discusses?

The Greek term used in this verse and rendered to 'speak against,' describes speech that expresses hostility, rejection, calumny. It also has the meaning of accusing someone, with, by implication, a false or exaggerated basis for the accusation.* (Compare its use at 1 Peter 2:12.) The fact that James goes on to speak of 'judging' one's brother and continues to deal with judging, winding up his discussion with the question, "Who are you to

---

* *Theological Dictionary of the New Testament*, Vol. IV, p. 3.

be judging your neighbor?" indicates that the 'speaking against one's brother' is a finding fault with him, being harshly critical of him, censuring him, but without genuine justification. This amounts to an expression of judgment of the brother, either of his person, his ways or his motives. It is an assessing of his moral worth in an adverse way that is unwarranted.* The wrong is compounded if this condemnatory speech is done behind the back of the one accused.

So, as regards the word "or" in the phrase "speaks against a brother or judges his brother," Greek scholar Lenski states: " 'Or' is conjunctive and not disjunctive," that is, it indicates that the 'speaking against' and the 'judging' are *related,* not disconnected, actions.

speaks against law and judges law

James states that such unjust, harsh and unkind criticism of one's Christian brother amounts to a speaking against law and a judging of it. Earlier in his letter James refers to the "kingly law" of loving one's neighbor and of "the law of a free people." (Jas. 2:8, 12) So it appears that, in the section under consideration, James is not referring to the Mosaic law but to God's law generally as it applied to the Christian congregation. As scholar Lenski points out, the word "law" in Greek is here anarthrous, that is, without the definite article "the," and this lends support to the view that James is not referring specifically to the Mosaic law (*"the* law"). It may be noted, however, that the "kingly law" of loving one's neighbor was also implicit in the Law covenant. Jesus in fact said that the whole Law (given through Moses to Israel) rested on but two commandments,

---

* The *Septuagint* translation uses the same Greek term in rendering Psalm 50:20: "You sit and speak against your brother, against the son of your mother you give away a fault." Other texts where the *Septuagint* uses this term are: Numbers 12:8; 21:5, 7; Job 19:3; Psalm 44:16; 78:19; 101:5.

love of God and love of one's neighbor. (Compare Leviticus 19:18; Matthew 22:37-40; Romans 13: 8-10.) Similarly, the "new commandment" given by Jesus also places its emphasis on such love. (John 13:34; 15:12) All the inspired Christian writings maintain that emphasis.

How, then, is the action described here a speaking against and a judging of law? We may find some parallel to this in what Jesus made clear in his condemnation of the scribes and Pharisees. They spoke against him and against his disciples, accusing them of lacking godly devotion, of being wrongly motivated, of doing acts that were unrighteous, such as violating the Sabbath. But they did this on the basis of standards that they themselves had set up (as in accusing the disciples of eating with "defiled hands"), or by stretching God's laws to an extreme point (as in condemning the picking, rubbing and eating of grain done on the Sabbath by the disciples). Jesus told them that they were "letting go the commandment of God [in order to] hold fast the tradition of men," and that they made "the word of God invalid" by the traditions that they handed down and that they used as a basis for judging. (Mark 7:1-9, 13; Luke 6:1, 2; 11:38; 14:1, 3; John 9:16) They had "seated themselves in the seat of Moses," who was specially used by Jehovah as lawgiver and judge for Israel; and, while zealously declaring what was recorded in God's law, they proceeded to add to this and lay upon the people many burdensome traditions. (Matt. 23:1-4; Acts 7: 35-38) Because the common people did not keep the Law according to *their* standards, they viewed these "as nothing" in their moral worth and judged them as "accursed." (Luke 18:9-12; John 7:49)

By doing this they were speaking against law and judging it. They presumed to have the prerogative and authority to give it their own interpretation, to expand it, or to emphasize one part to the neglect of the other.* Jesus told them that they scrupled at minor matters and showed little concern for major ones, that they "disregarded the weightier matters of the Law, namely, justice and mercy and faithfulness." (Matt. 23:16-24) At Matthew 7:1-5 Jesus instructed his disciples to avoid such a wrong course of judging their brothers.

In yet another way, speaking against one's brother (perhaps in a backbiting way), or judging him, is 'speaking against law,' in that it does not contribute to good order and peace. Psalm 119:165 says: "Abundant peace belongs to those loving your law." Harsh criticism and unjust judging, if carried on by many in a congregation, could lead to virtual anarchy. The result would be as the apostle Paul, after counseling those in the Galatian congregations to love one another, warned: "If, though, you keep on biting and devouring one another, look out that you do not get annihilated by one another." (Gal. 5:13-15)

Thus James' counsel was certainly needed. In the Christian congregation in Rome, for example, there were problems due to the practice of making "decisions on inward questionings [discriminations of reasonings, *Kingdom Interlinear*]."† Those whose consciences allowed them to do certain things and to refrain from doing others were 'looking down' on those whose consciences did not so allow, while the latter were 'judging' the former as engaging in a wrongful course. (Rom. 14:1-3) Rather than taking it upon themselves to criticize and judge others, Paul urged them to be controlled and motivated by love, avoiding, out of

* Rabbinical writings demonstrate that these prominent ones viewed it as within their province and duty to rule on virtually any aspect of the lives and activities of their Jewish brothers.

† Other renderings are: "arguing over [personal] scruples," Phillips' *The New Testament in Modern English;* "passing judgment on disputable matters," *New International Version.*

concern for their brothers' spiritual welfare, those things that would cause stumbling or tripping. (Rom. 14:13-15, 19-21; 15:1-3; compare 1 Corinthians 8:4, 7-13.)

James' counsel harmonizes with that of Paul. In no way is the Christian prohibited from having his own view, even a firm view, in such matters for personal decision. What is condemned is not the forming of our own judgment, but it is our using such personal view or decision as the basis for accusing and judging our brother. (Compare Romans 14:5, 22, 23.) If we do this we elevate ourselves over our brother as judge; we view ourselves as his superior, with the right to overrule his personal decision in such matters and to condemn him. (Compare 1 Corinthians 10:29, 30.)

Now if you judge law, you are, not a doer of law, but a judge

A Christian's duty is to obey God's law, not to set himself up as a critic. Since the Law commands love toward one's brother, as well as toward others, if a person harshly criticizes his brother and judges him, he is not loving him and thereby he is, not a doer, but an offender against the "kingly law." (Compare Ephesians 4:31, 32; 5:1, 2.) Not only this, but he, in effect, removes himself from the common level of those who are subject to the law and elevates himself to the superior position of judge.

His 'judging of law' may be in a number of ways. In not viewing *all* its commands—including loving one's neighbor and refraining from unjustly accusing him—as binding upon him, he thus judges part of the law as not worthy of his obedience. In condemning his brother in matters in which God's law does not condemn, he is, in effect, judging*

---

* In connection with this text, the Schaff-Lange Bible commentary observes: "Whosoever burdens his neighbour with arbitrary commandments, pronounces upon the deficiency of the Christian doctrine and in so far sets himself up as its judge."

12 One there is that is lawgiver and judge, he who is able to save and to destroy. But you, who are you to be judging your neighbor?

---

that law as being inadequate, unable to perform properly its service as the basis for judging, hence, as not written as it should have been and needing the additions or adjustments that he would make. In James' day, some Christians wanted to hold to observances of the Jewish law and, at times, these criticized and spoke against their brothers who did not. In so doing they were finding fault with the "law of a free people," of which James speaks. They judged the setting aside of the Mosaic Law code as unwise, improper, as likely to contribute to looseness and wrongdoing. (Compare Colossians 2:16, 17, 20-23; Hebrews 8:10-13.)

12 One there is that is lawgiver and judge, he who is able to save and to destroy

James now goes further and shows the enormity of the wrong involved in this unjust incriminating of one's brother. Since the one doing this makes himself a judge of God's law, he thereby places himself on the same level of authority as the *source* of that law, the lawgiver. In his unjust judging of his brother, such a one, in effect, may even presume to introduce his own legislation, based on his own personal standards. But James states the truth that there is but *one* lawgiver and judge. This is not some human, but Jehovah God, the Supreme Judge and Lawgiver. (Isa. 33:22) He alone has the sovereign right to set the standards and rules for salvation, since he alone is "able to save and to destroy," able to reward fully and to punish fully. God's Son said: "Do not become fearful of those who kill the body but cannot kill the soul; but rather be in fear of him that can destroy both soul and body in Gehenna."

(Matt. 10:28; compare Psalm 68:20; 75:7.)
Though the one speaking against and judging his
brother may not be fully aware of the reality and
the enormity of the position he assumes, what a
perilous position he occupies in trying to take on
the judicial functions of the infallible God!

"The law of Jehovah is perfect"; hence, it is
complete, refined, not deficient, inadequate or in-
competent as to accomplishing its designed purpose. (Ps. 19:7) The Israelites were told by God:
"Every word that I am commanding you is what
you should be careful to do. You must not add
to it nor take away from it." (Deut. 12:32; compare Proverbs 30:5, 6; Revelation 22:18.) "Your
law is truth," says Psalm 119:142, and so it is in
accord with the real state of things and is *right*
for what is actually needed. Being the sole Legis-
lator and Judge, God alone can decide when to
set aside any of his legislation as having served
its purpose (as he did with the Law covenant), or
to bring in new commandments and legislation.
(Heb. 8:10-13; compare Galatians 1:8, 9, 11, 12.)
Just as it would be the height of disrespect for
humans to endeavor to make God's law appear to
approve that which it condemns, so, too, it would
be equally presumptuous to make it appear to
forbid what it allows. (Isa. 5:20; Prov. 17:15)
The Jewish religious leaders, despite their zeal
for the Law code, were guilty of this. James
shows that his brothers in the Christian congregation needed to guard against committing a
similar error.

But you, who are you to be judging your neigh-bor?

James' question is devastatingly forceful. It indeed seems incredible that any frail, erring, imperfect, sinful human would view it as within his
right and province to act in the place of the infallible God by judging a fellow human, when

13 Come, now, you who say: "Today or tomorrow we will journey to this city and will spend a year there, and we will engage in business and make profits,"

God, by his Word, has not done so. God's perfect, sinless Son stated repeatedly his careful, faithful adherence to what his Father had said, and his firm refusal to take action or make judgments of his own originality. (John 5:30, 45; 7:16-24; 8:15, 16, 26, 28; 12:28-50) He tells us as disciples that if we, as imperfect, sinful creatures, do not want to be judged and condemned ourselves, then we should not take it upon ourselves arbitrarily to judge and condemn our neighbor. (Matt. 7:1-5; Luke 6:37; compare Romans 2:1-3.)

James' question finds a parallel in that of the apostle Paul at Romans 14:4: "Who are you to judge the house servant of another? To his own master he stands or falls." It is the master's right to lay down the laws for his own servant, to impose duties and restrictions upon him, to retain or discharge him. To anyone presuming to take on this responsibility, the master of the servant would rightly say: 'Just who do you think you are?' (Compare Proverbs 30:10; 1 Corinthians 4:1-5.) That being so, the apostle goes on to say: "But why do you judge your brother? Or why do you also look down on your brother? For we shall all stand before the judgment seat of God." (Rom. 14:10; see also verses 11 through 13.) Recognition of God's impartiality in judgment and of our own weaknesses will help us to avoid feelings of self-righteousness and superiority toward our neighbor. (Compare Job 31:13-15.)

13 Come, now, you who say: "Today or tomorrow we will journey to this city and will spend a year

there, and we will engage in business and make profits"

James here addresses those who make such plans to the disregard of God and the life they

Avoid Boastful Self-Confidence

should be living in devotion to him. This parallels his warning in verses 1-10 about disregarding God for friendship with the world, and in verses 11, 12 about ignoring God as judge and lawgiver. These people speak as if having prophetic knowledge of the future, with their whole purpose centered on their business schemes. They even have it all figured out how long they will be in the distant city and the profits they will make. Such restless changing of locations makes it difficult for a Christian to do good work in teaching the Bible to people and in helping them spiritually.

However, James does not condemn the traveling, but, rather, the *spirit* of these people in their presumptuous, self-confident assertions. They do not take into consideration Jesus' parable of the foolish rich man who, planning for greatly expanded financial ventures, never even lived

14 whereas you do not know what your life will be tomorrow. For you are a mist appearing for a little while and then disappearing. **15** Instead, you ought to say: "If Jehovah wills, we shall live and also do this or that."

---

the next day. This man 'laid up treasure for himself but was not rich toward God.' (Luke 12: 16-21)

14 whereas you do not know what your life will be tomorrow

The proverb counsels: "Do not make your boast about the next day, for you do not know what a day will give birth to." (Prov. 27:1) No man knows what the next day will bring, not even the next minute. Actually, he may not be alive the next minute. Only God knows the future. Neither those to whom James spoke, nor any persons to-day, have been gifted with prophetic insight. Rather, "time and unforeseen occurrence befall them all." (Eccl. 9:11, 12)

For you are a mist appearing for a little while and then disappearing

Life is like a vapor, like a morning mist that is evanescent, dissolving as we watch it. We are therefore foolish to view life in this system of things as substantial, something on which we can confidently build. (Eccl. 1:2; 2:17, 18) It is not logical thus to ignore the true state of affairs, and especially to neglect God and what he says. The patriarch Job expressed himself similarly: "Remember that my life is wind." And David acknowledged to God: "Like a shadow our days are upon the earth." (Job 7:7; 1 Chron. 29:15; compare Psalm 90:9, 10.)

15 Instead, you ought to say: "If Jehovah wills, we shall live and also do this or that"

16 But now you take pride in your self-assuming brags. All such taking of pride is wicked.

James is not speaking about using the expression "If Jehovah wills" in business matters, as if to place the responsibility upon Jehovah for success or failure in the venture. But, actually, in any matter, work or venture, one genuinely saying "If Jehovah wills" is also trying to do the things that are according to Jehovah's will. It may be necessary to do business, or to travel to a place for such a purpose, in order to carry out Christian obligations, such as caring for one's family. Of course, Jehovah God *never* wills that we do something out of wholly mercenary, selfish motives, though he may not prevent us from doing it. But whatever we do, we should recognize that nothing adverse to us can take place unless Jehovah permits it. If we do not neglect God in our decisions and plans, we will always be safe, whether our plans are carried out as we thought, or not. The apostle Paul kept this principle closely in mind. (Acts 18:21; 1 Cor. 4:19; 16:7; Heb. 6:3) A Christian who acknowledges Jehovah in all his ways will experience the fulfillment of the Lord's Prayer, "do not bring us into temptation," because he will not ignore the warnings God brings to his attention and will look to God for guidance. (Matt. 6:13)

However, we do not want to adopt the expression "If Jehovah wills" as a cliché, something repeated out of a superstitious feeling, or from custom or habit, merely to impress our listeners. This becomes hypocritical and a mockery of the principle. (Compare Matthew 6:5-8.) The sincere person does not necessarily make the statement audibly, but may often do so in his heart.

16 But now you take pride in your self-assuming

17 Therefore, if one knows how to do what is right and yet does not do it, it is a sin for him.

---

brags. All such taking of pride is wicked

They were exulting in illusions. We have heard businessmen of the world bragging about the maneuvers and deals they plan to carry out, but Christians should not have that attitude. Such boasters are acting as if they could control the future. They are trying to appear to be something that they are not. The word translated "self-assuming brags" is the word used at 1 John 2:16 and there translated "showy display" (of one's means of life).

Such taking of pride is wicked, because it is founded on a wrong view of oneself and of what may occur. It ignores our dependence upon God. (Jer. 9:23, 24) This thinking is grounded in self-delusion and haughtiness. It is therefore wicked. The Christian, by avoiding such an attitude, will be avoiding condemnation by God.

17 Therefore, if one knows how to do what is right and yet does not do it, it is a sin for him

This statement by James is evidently a conclusion to what he has just said about self-assumption and vain boasting, neglecting our complete dependence upon God. Jehovah requires humility and the acknowledgment of him as the source of life and all good things; and we must recognize that we can accomplish nothing lasting without his favor and help. If a Christian knows this and does not act accordingly, it is a sin to him.

But James' words can have broader application. Many are the parables and statements in God's Word that emphasize the seriousness of sins of omission. (Luke 12:47, 48) In Jesus' parable of the sheep and the goats, the goats are condemned, not for any specific bad, illegal or immoral thing that they did, but for not helping Christ's brothers when they had opportunity. (Matt. 25:41-46; compare 1 John 3:15-17; Proverbs 3:27, 28.) The wicked slave in the parable of the talents is not accused of doing anything forbidden, but of not using the talent committed to him as he should have done. He merely buried it and returned it without gain to his master. He did not use it for the purpose for which it was committed to him. (Matt. 25:24-27) In the illustration about the rich man and Lazarus, the rich man is not charged with specifically doing something unlawful. Rather, he failed to use his riches in the right way. (Luke 16:19-21, 25)

Close self-examination is required on the part of all Christians, for it is sometimes easier to avoid doing something that we should not do than it is to exert ourselves and do the things that we know we should do.

QUESTIONS FOR STUDY

VERSE 1
From what source are there wars and from what source are there fights among you?
  1 What was the condition among Christians to whom James wrote?

Are they not from this source, namely, from your cravings for sensual pleasure that carry on a conflict in your members?
  1 What was the source of the problem?
  2 How did the cravings for sensual pleasure work in the congregation, and to what extent did it carry them?
  3 Name some of the things that should be classified as 'sensual pleasures.'
  4 Within the Christian himself what activity does the sinful flesh carry on?
  5 What will the person who allows fleshly cravings to overcome him do in the congregation?

VERSE 2

You desire, and yet you do not have

    1 Though James did not specify, what may he have meant by saying: "and yet you do not have"?

    2 How does another Bible translation give a cause-and-result application to this part of the verse?

You go on murdering and coveting

    1 To what extent were some members of the congregations allowing the cravings for sensual pleasure to go?

    2 How were some Christians showing a greedy and hateful spirit toward their brothers?

    3 How is such selfish spirit closely related to murder?

and yet you are not able to obtain

    1 Why could the ones having the desire not obtain the desired things?

You go on fighting and waging war

    1 Why did they go on fighting?

    2 Can such things actually take place in a congregation today? What would prevent it?

You do not have because of your not asking

    1 Why did they not ask God to grant the things desired?

    2 What should they have asked for, and would these things have been granted by God?

VERSE 3

You do ask, and yet you do not receive

    1 When they did ask, why were their prayers not answered?

because you are asking for a wrong purpose, that you may expend it upon your cravings for sensual pleasure

    1 What factors were wrong about what they were requesting?

    2 When they asked, what were they actually requesting God to do for them?

    3 How did God view such prayers?

    4 Into what state were these persons in danger of falling?

    5 How does one Bible commentary sum up the principle expressed by James in the opening part of this chapter?

VERSE 4

Adulteresses

    1 How is the Christian congregation viewed in the Scriptures?

    2 How do examples in the Hebrew Scriptures show us what is meant by James' use of the term "adulter-

esses" when he is speaking to certain ones in the Christian congregation?

do you not know that the friendship with the world is enmity with God?

1 Why did James use the question form in this sentence?

2 How is friendship with the world enmity with God?

3 In what way does a Christian manifest friendship with the world?

Whoever, therefore, wants to be a friend of the world is constituting himself an enemy of God

1 What change would a Christian have to make in order to become a friend of the world?

2 What attitude toward God are those becoming friends of the world displaying?

VERSE 5

Or does it seem to you that the scripture says to no purpose

1 Is there any scripture that says precisely what James says about the tendency to envy?

"It is with a tendency to envy that the spirit which has taken up residence within us keeps longing"

1 How does this agree with Genesis 8:21, and what example do we have to prove this?

2 Why was it not without purpose that the Scriptures speak against envy?

3 How is the tendency to envy demonstrated in the world?

4 What is the sense that the word "longing" conveys?

5 What can be said of other translations of James 4:5, and what meaning would such renderings convey?

VERSE 6

However, the undeserved kindness which he gives is greater

1 How can the force God provides counteract our inborn leaning toward envy?

2 How does God give undeserved kindness with a force greater than the forces working against the Christian?

Hence it says

1 By "it," to what does James here refer?

God opposes the haughty ones, but he gives undeserved kindness to the humble ones

1 Why and how does God give undeserved kindness to the humble ones?

VERSE 7

Subject yourselves, therefore, to God
   1 To what extent should Christians subject them-
      selves to God?

but oppose the Devil
   1 What things does one who opposes the Devil have
      to "stand against"?

and he will flee from you
   1 What is essential to Christians in order that they
      may resist the Devil successfully?
   2 How can the Christian rest assured that he will win
      out by resisting the Devil?

VERSE 8

Draw close to God, and he will draw close to you
   1 How do Christians draw close to God?

*Cleanse your hands, you sinners, and purify your hearts,
you indecisive ones*
   1 In what way were those to whom James addressed
      these words "sinners"?
   2 Why did they need to cleanse their hands and
      purify their hearts?
   3 In what way were these persons "indecisive"?
   4 Why should this counsel cause us to think seriously
      about ourselves?

VERSE 9

Give way to misery and mourn and weep
   1 Was James counseling Christians to be joyless,
      presenting a mournful appearance, or what?

*Let your laughter be turned into mourning, and your
joy into dejection*
   1 How does Paul describe the sadness that the Chris-
      tian should have, in contrast with the way the world
      usually has sadness?
   2 How did the conflict in his members help the apostle
      Paul spiritually?
   3 What spirit did James want the brothers to have?

VERSE 10

*Humble yourselves in the eyes of Jehovah, and he will
exalt you*
   1 Why must we humble ourselves in the eyes of
      Jehovah?
   2 How do we see this principle in the action of the
      prodigal son and the tax collector?
   3 In what condition can we make an acceptable sacri-
      fice to God, and how will he exalt us?

VERSE 11

Quit speaking against one another, brothers
1 What may have been the source of the problem James now considers?
2 What kind of spirit may a person have, and what is he often trying to accomplish, in speaking against another Christian?

He who speaks against a brother or judges his brother
1 Why does this not rule out the reproving and condemning of those engaging in sinful conduct?
2 What kind of adverse speech is here involved, and how is it related to judging?

speaks against law and judges law
1 Of what "law" does James here speak?
2 On what does such law place prime emphasis?
3 What helpful example is there showing how such speech is a judging of law?
4 How does the effect of such speech on a congregation also show it is 'against law'?
5 What situation in the congregation in Rome illustrates the need of this counsel?
6 What is, and what is not, condemned by this counsel?

Now if you judge law, you are, not a doer of law, but a judge
1 In what ways do those speaking against their brother cease to be 'doers of law'?
2 In what various ways could the Christian make himself a judge of law?

VERSE 12

One there is that is lawgiver and judge, he who is able to save and to destroy
1 What makes the wrong course described so reprehensible?
2 Why is Jehovah rightly the only "lawgiver and judge" as regards the requirements for salvation?
3 What is the proper attitude to show toward Jehovah's law?

But you, who are you to be judging your neighbor?
1 Why is this question so devastatingly forceful?
2 How did God's Son provide the right example and counsel?
3 How do the apostle Paul's statements in Romans chapter 14 contribute to our understanding of the point?

VERSE 13

Come, now, you who say: "Today or tomorrow we will

journey to this city and will spend a year there, and we will engage in business and make profits"

   1 Is James here condemning the traveling and the business venture in themselves?

   2 What are these men doing that James warns against?

   3 What parable of Jesus emphasized this same principle?

VERSE 14

whereas you do not know what your life will be tomorrow

   1 How does this statement show that the boaster is wrong?

For you are a mist appearing for a little while and then disappearing

   1 Why is it foolish to view life in this system of things as substantial?

VERSE 15

Instead, you ought to say: "If Jehovah wills, we shall live and also do this or that"

   1 In entering upon a work or project, why is it proper to say "If Jehovah wills, we shall live and also do this or that"?

   2 What attitude will one who genuinely says "If Jehovah wills" have as to the outcome of the thing he is doing?

   3 If one enters upon a work with the genuine feeling that if Jehovah wills it will prosper, what will he properly do as he is carrying out the work?

   4 What is one doing who audibly voices the expression "If Jehovah wills" in every little affair of life?

VERSE 16

But now you take pride in your self-assuming brags. All such taking of pride is wicked

   1 What brags do some commercially minded persons make, and why?

   2 Why is such taking of pride wicked?

VERSE 17

Therefore, if one knows how to do what is right and yet does not do it, it is a sin for him

   1 To what does James evidently refer by this statement?

   2 How bad are the sins of omission?

   3 Why does this chapter of James require self-examination on the part of all Christians?

CHAPTER 5

1 Come, now, you rich men, weep, howling over your miseries that are coming upon you.

---

1 Come, now, you rich men

James calls special attention to a certain class of men—the rich who use their riches *wrongly*.

Warning to the Rich Not all rich persons fall into this category. In James 1:10 he speaks of the Christian brother who is humble though rich. (Compare 1 Timothy 6:17-19.) Despite the fact that it is difficult, a rich person may be saved. Besides finding it difficult for themselves, the rich class in general were to a great extent a source of trouble to Christians.

Why would these words addressed to such unjust rich persons be included in a letter to Christian congregations? Likely there were a few such ones within the congregations. But there may have been many who showed an inclination toward materialism or toward admiration of the wealthy class, even desiring to become like them. This may be indicated by the words just preceding this section (Jas. 4:13-16), as well as by the partial treatment some were giving to the rich man who came into their meetings. (Jas. 2:1-4)

James' addressing himself to the rich who misused their riches somewhat parallels what Jesus Christ did when speaking to his disciples on one occasion. After describing several happinesses these disciples should aim for, Jesus said: "Woe to you rich persons, because you are having your consolation in full." (Luke 6:20-25) Though the rich as a class obviously would not read his letter, James, by employing the literary device of direct address, was helping Christians to get the right viewpoint.

Christians might begin to view the prosperity of rich men with envy, becoming unappreciative, losing sight of their own wonderful relationship with God and developing discontentment. (Compare 1 Timothy 6:9, 10.) There was a danger of their becoming impatient because relief from the oppression by the wealthy class, through the execution of God's judgment, did not come as soon as they might desire. They might even become bitter, vengeful, and develop a bad spirit toward their fellowmen and God.

James writes, therefore, to correct his brothers' view and to comfort them. Psalm 73 was written by Asaph for the same reason. He says: "As for me, my feet had almost turned aside, my steps had nearly been made to slip. For I became envious of the boasters . . . their paunch is fat." (Vss. 2-4) He describes the material prosperity of these wicked ones, their apparent security and safety, and the success of their schemes. (Vss. 5-14) Then, he corrects his thinking and confesses how unreasonable he was and explains that he had overlooked God's viewpoint and God's judgment of the wicked, and the final blessing to those truly worshiping God. (Vss. 15-28)

weep, howling over your miseries that are coming upon you

This weeping is not the sorrow that accompanies repentance, but is the weeping of anguish in punishment, or in anticipation of it. It is the kind of sadness described as "the sadness of the world [that] produces death." (2 Cor. 7:10) The rich men who wickedly oppressed the Christians and others then and now must howl when God rewards them according to the deeds they have committed. If not before, this certainly comes on their day of judgment. These riches have often

2 Your riches have rotted, and your outer garments have become moth-eaten.

---

been obtained by fraud and oppression, or, if gained honestly, tended to develop in their owners a greedy spirit, and were often used in a wrong way. The possessors of riches often are self-deceived, thinking their riches to be a security. (Matt. 13:22; Ps. 144:11-15a) This condemnation is set out by James to prevent Christians from getting a false sense of values and also to comfort them in their comparative poverty, strengthening them to endure.

2 Your riches have rotted

Wealth in James' day consisted to a great extent of perishable materials, such as stores of grain, oil and wine. (Compare Luke 12:16-21; Joel 2:19.) These things James viewed as having rotted already. Of course, not all riches rot; James is speaking figuratively of their being useless, like something that has rotted. He is emphasizing, not the *perishableness* of wealth, but the *worthlessness* of it, as compared to the riches the Christian possesses. (Prov. 11:28)

and your outer garments have become moth-eaten

Garments were another item of

3 Your gold and silver are rusted away, and their rust will be as a witness against you and will eat your fleshy parts. Something like fire is what you have stored up in the last days.

---

riches. Some rich men had hundreds, even thousands of garments. These would be used to attire the man's guests on certain occasions, as in the parable of the marriage feast. (Matt. 22:11; compare Matthew 6:19.) There is an account in the writings of the Roman poet Horace that when a wealthy man named Lucullus was requested to lend 100 garments for the theater, he replied that he had 5,000 in the house, to which they were welcome.* Likely many of these had already been attacked by moths.

3 Your gold and silver are rusted away

The Greek word here is, literally, "rusted." Gold and silver do not actually rust, but James figuratively says that the gold and silver are as valueless as something that has rusted, that is of no use but to be thrown away. Gold, and particularly silver, takes on a darker, unburnished or tarnished look with age.

and their rust will be as a witness against you

The fact that the gold and the silver have not been put to a good use, but have been hoarded up and allowed to "rust," stands as a witness. The accumulated "rust" gives proof as to the non-use of these riches.

and will eat your fleshy parts

Those who have tied up all their hopes and interests in wealth now find that same wealth working against them, accusing them. Like a rusty chain that wears away at the flesh, cor-

* Albert Barnes, *Notes* on James 5:2.

4 Look! The wages due the workers who harvested your fields but which are held up by you, keep crying out, and the calls for help on the part of the reapers have entered into the ears of Jehovah of armies.

---

roding and thus consuming it, this adverse witness progressively destroys their attractive fleshed-up appearance and leads to their ultimate death as a hideous corpse. (Compare Psalm 73:4-20; Revelation 17:16; 19:17, 18.)

Something like fire is what you have stored up in the last days

Since the time when Christ walked the earth, all men are called upon to listen to the "good news" and to repent. The apostle Paul said to a group of men at Athens: "True, God has overlooked the times of such ignorance [as the idolatry of the pagan nations], yet now he is telling mankind that they should all everywhere repent." (Acts 17:30) Those who trust in their material possessions are now storing up and relying on their treasure, and will no doubt have the same spirit when God's day of judgment comes upon them. Then it will bring the fire of his anger against them. (Compare Isaiah 30:27.) The apostle Paul likewise speaks to certain inexcusable ones, saying: "According to your hardness and unrepentant heart you are storing up wrath for yourself on the day of wrath and of the revealing of God's righteous judgment." (Rom. 2:5; note Ezekiel 7:19; Zephaniah 1:18.)

4 Look! The wages due the workers who harvested your fields but which are held up by you, keep crying out

The harvesttime is when the greatest wealth would be brought in. Even at this most prosperous

5 You have lived in luxury upon the earth and have gone in for sensual pleasure. You have fattened your hearts on the day of slaughter.

---

time, the rich greedily withheld the wages of those who did the work of harvesting. (Compare Jeremiah 22:13, 17.) These wages of which the workers were defrauded are said to "keep crying out" for God to act in vengeance, as did Abel's blood. (Gen. 4:9, 10) This verse would, of course, apply to the defrauding of workers in any occupation, or even to slaves, who, though not paid wages, were morally entitled to some benefits from their labors.

and the calls for help on the part of the reapers have entered into the ears of Jehovah of armies

The workers themselves also complain and cry out, whether directly to God or not, for justice. God, who sees all things and who is a champion of the oppressed, made special mention of this situation in the Mosaic law, stating: "You must not defraud a hired laborer who is in trouble and poor, whether of your brothers or of your alien residents who are in your land, within your gates. In his day you should give him his wages, and the sun should not set upon them, because he is in trouble and is lifting up his soul to his wages; that he may not cry out to Jehovah against you, and it must become sin on your part." (Deut. 24:14, 15) Jehovah of armies, meaning the God who has all the hosts of heavenly angels at his command, and who controls all things in the universe, hears these cries for help, and he will answer them. (Compare Genesis 18:20.) Into what great peril the defrauders place themselves!

5 You have lived in luxury upon the earth

They have desired and used their riches so that

they can live in indulgence and ease, soft luxury. The expression 'living in luxury' does not necessarily mean that they lived immorally or committed wrong acts openly, but that they lived for their own enjoyment, heedless of the needs of others. (Compare the attitude of the rich man, at Luke 12:19, and the people before the flood of Noah's day. [Matt. 24:38, 39])

and have gone in for sensual pleasure

The Greek word rendered "sensual pleasure" implies voluptuous living, even to the point of wastefulness. These rich men's thoughts were entirely fleshly, not spiritual. They were 'given over' to this pattern of life. The apostle Paul used a similar expression in saying (about widows): "The one that goes in for sensual gratification is dead though she is living." (1 Tim. 5:6) Such a mental attitude and the love of pleasure often lead to actual immorality, not just sexual, but immorality of various kinds. (Compare 2 Timothy 3:2-6.) Among these could be acts of oppression and cruelty in order to gain and retain wealth so as to perpetuate their luxurious style of living.

You have fattened your hearts on the day of slaughter

James means the day of slaughter that is to come. On this very "day," destined for their slaughter, they keep right on 'fattening their hearts.' They build up fatty hearts, denoting overindulgence in sensual pleasure. What they are doing is building up an adverse judgment for themselves on that day. They are like cattle eating all that they can, fattened, ready for the slaughter, though they do not know it. (Compare Psalm 49: 6, 7, 10-13.) A day of judgment is sometimes called a time of slaughter. (Isa. 34:2, 6; Ezek. 21:10, 15)

6 You have condemned, you have murdered the righteous one. Is he not opposing you?

---

6 You have condemned, you have murdered the righteous one

The "righteous one" apparently has reference to followers of Jesus Christ, the righteous One. (Acts 7:52; 22:14) James possibly had in mind the murder of Jesus Christ by the rich and prominent leaders of the Jews. The Sanhedrin, the Jewish high court that sentenced Jesus to death, likely had in its ranks many such men. Nevertheless, James is here speaking of those wicked rich persons who were at that very moment oppressing Christians, and likened their persecution and murder of Christians to this most enormous crime of all time. (Compare Matthew 25:40-45.) The psalmist wrote: "The wicked one is plotting against the righteous one, and at him he is grinding his teeth. Jehovah himself will laugh at him, for he certainly sees that his day will come. The wicked ones have drawn a sword itself and have bent their bow, to cause the afflicted and poor one to fall, to slaughter those who are upright in their way." "The wicked one is keeping on the watch for the righteous and is seeking to put him to death." (Ps. 37:12-14, 32)

Is he not opposing you?

The righteous ones do stand firm for what is right, though, of course, they are unable to put a stop to the oppression they undergo at the hands of such unjust rich ones. However, the word here translated "opposing" is a term implying strong or formidable resistance; there is an adversary relationship implied. (Compare James 4:6: "God *opposes* the haughty ones"; Romans 13:2: "He who *opposes* the authority has taken a stand against the arrangement of God"; Acts 18:6:

"They kept on *opposing* and speaking abusively." In these passages a form of the same word is used.) Literally, the phrase, then, can be rendered: "Is he not ranging himself up against you?" (*Kingdom Interlinear Translation*)

An alternate rendering of this verse after the words "righteous one" could be: "He is not opposing you."* This would correspond with the counsel of Jesus at Matthew 5:39: "Do not resist him that is wicked."

When Jesus was on trial before the Sanhedrin and later before Pilate, he stood firm for the truth and for God's kingdom, as well as for his legal rights. Yet he never resisted in the sense of fighting back or slandering or reviling his persecutors. (John 18:19-23, 33-38; 1 Pet. 2:23) To the contrary, he was like a sheep led to the slaughter. (Isa. 53:7) Paul also defended himself with available legal means and spoke fearlessly before authorities, yet he was never guilty of deliberate disrespect or insubordination. (Acts 16:35-39; 25:11; 26:1, 2) In all cases then, there was no justification for the persecuting of such ones on the basis of any fighting against duly constituted authority or of the existing order of things within which the rich ones functioned.

Although the righteous course of God's servants may seem in vain, this is never the case. For the record of the poor and righteous who have been oppressed and even murdered will be a witness against the wicked oppressors in the day of God's judgment. Jesus said that when his disciples would be delivered up to kings, governors and courts and scourged, this would constitute a witness to them and the nations. (Matt. 10:18; Mark 13:9) The

---

* See footnote on James 5:6 in the large-print edition of the *New World Translation*. Some other renderings are: "You have condemned and murdered innocent men, who were not opposing you." (*New International Version*) "It was you who condemned the innocent and killed them; they offered you no resistance." (*The Jerusalem Bible*)

7 Exercise patience, therefore, brothers, until the presence of the Lord. Look! The farmer keeps waiting for the precious fruit of the earth, exercising patience over it until he gets the early rain and the late rain.

---

murderers of the righteous one, therefore, do not get by without having the testimony and warning given by the righteous one as to the badness of their acts.

7 Exercise patience, therefore, brothers, until the presence of the Lord

James had described the sins that the rich as a class were committing against the righteous, these being (1) hoarding up money that could be used to help the poor; (2) holding up the wages that were urgently needed by those harvesting the fields; (3) living greedily in luxury, and with pleasure as their aim; and (4) condemning and murdering the righteous one. Now James speaks to comfort the oppressed Christians and to encourage them to be patient, not becoming discontented and giving out, not becoming irritable against one another, and not letting evil destroy their steadfast continuance in doing God's will.

Encouragement to Patience

James exhorts the brothers to bear with patience the things that come upon them not only from wealthy oppressors and others but also from the hardships that come in everyday life. He calls attention to the thing that would bring them the only real and lasting relief, namely, the presence of the Lord. This was certainly worth waiting for with patient endurance. Those living in the first century were to die before that time came, but their patient endurance under hardships until the end of their lifetime would establish for them a good record with God. During the *parousia*, or "presence of the Lord," judgment would come upon their oppressors and bring reward to them. (Matt. 24:3, 37-39)

Look! The farmer keeps waiting for the precious fruit of the earth

The farmer has no control over the weather or the growth of his plants, but he is sure of the progression of the seasons. He knows that it is God who makes his crop grow, and that he cannot

hasten the day of harvest, though he looks forward with anticipation to the precious life-sustaining fruit for himself and his family. (Compare 1 Corinthians 3:7.)

exercising patience over it until he gets the early rain and the late rain

In Palestine, the early rain came about planting time, in the fall. The late rain came in the spring, enabling the crop to come to full, abundant fruitage—the thing for which the farmer waits. (Joel 2:23; Zech. 10:1)

8 You too exercise patience; make your hearts firm, because the presence of the Lord has drawn close.

9 Do not heave sighs against one another, brothers, so that you do not get judged. Look! The Judge is standing before the doors.

---

8 You too exercise patience; make your hearts firm, because the presence of the Lord has drawn close

The things that were happening to Christians should never be allowed to shake their firmness in Christ. Their hope, based on a sure foundation, is that relief *will* come. More than that, it will be a time of accounting for all. (Rom. 9:28; Matt. 16:27) Whether they individually lived until that time or not, their own keeping of firm hearts, and faithful, patient waiting for their Lord were what would count; if they lost their patience and failed to endure, they would lose out on the blessings to be brought during the Lord's presence.

9 Do not heave sighs against one another, brothers

Christians are told here not to groan or sigh deeply with regard to one another. The Greek term here used could have a sense of an inner sighing or groaning, not an open expression of dissatisfaction or complaint. (Compare its use at Romans 8:23.) James earlier had written about a Christian's speaking against his brothers and judging them. But here he deals with the very *feeling* shown toward one's brothers, which can strongly affect the spirit manifested toward them. When disappointed once or repeatedly in another person, we may heave a sigh against such a person who fails to fulfill our expectations or wishes. So James is telling his readers not to become vexed with their Christian brothers and express their vexation with groaning or sighing deeply. They should realize that disappointing or vexatious things will take place in the present imperfect system of things. The tensions and frustrations of this system cause people to make mistakes and demonstrate traits that are undesirable. But the Christian, knowing this, should control his own spirit and be merciful and considerate with others, particularly his Christian brothers. (Compare Galatians 6:10.) Rather than become fretful, ill-humored or negative, letting his feelings toward his brothers become soured, he will strive to show long-suffering and maintain the joy and the cheerful spirit that should distinguish the one hoping in God's kingdom and producing the fruitage of His spirit. (Compare Romans 14:17; Galatians 5:22; Philippians 2:19.)

so that you do not get judged

James warns that, if they indulge in groaning and heaving sighs against one another, they themselves will be found guilty and will be judged accordingly. They will be condemned by the Judge who sees and knows the innermost workings of the heart. Groaning or sighing of itself is not what is condemned, for Jesus also sighed deeply. (Mark 7:34; see also 2 Corinthians 5:2, 4.) But if the groaning or heaving of sighs is motivated by a wrong heart attitude toward one's brother, such reaction forebodes ill for such a one.

Look! The Judge is standing before the doors

By this illustration James is indicating that the coming of the Lord Jesus Christ is near at hand. For example, at Mark 13:29 Jesus spoke with reference to the end of the system of things and said: "Likewise also you, when you see these things happening, know that he is near, at the doors." Hence, since James warned the Christians of the first century about the nearness of the

10 Brothers, take as a pattern of the suffering of evil and the exercising of patience the prophets, who spoke in the name of Jehovah.

---

coming of the Lord Jesus Christ as Judge, much more should we of this 20th century take under serious consideration the nearness of the Lord's coming for the purpose of rendering final judgment. We might be suddenly overtaken by him when we are improperly groaning or heaving deep sighs against our Christian brothers. We must never let our longing for relief through the Lord's coming gradually give way to impatience and, in consequence, feel dissatisfaction toward our Christian brothers. Though no words may be voiced, a person's heart attitude can condemn him. (Compare Matthew 5:28; 1 John 3:15.)

10 Brothers, take as a pattern of the suffering of evil and the exercising of patience the prophets, who spoke in the name of Jehovah

The prophets of old spoke as Jehovah directed them by his spirit and according to his revelations. James encourages the brothers to follow in the path that the prophets trod, a fine, satisfying path but also one with severely rough places. He implies that the course of God's servants was always one calling for faith and endurance. All the prophets suffered evil, even at the hands of their own countrymen—those who professed to be worshipers of God. Jeremiah was an outstanding example of a servant of God suffering all kinds of afflictions but continuing his prophetic work in patient endurance. (Jer. 20:8-11) The Christian martyr Stephen said to the Jewish religious leaders: "Which one of the prophets did your forefathers not persecute?" (Acts 7:52)

These faithful prophets at times felt discouraged, perplexed. But they never abandoned their

11 Look! We pronounce happy those who have endured. You have heard of the endurance of Job and have seen the outcome Jehovah gave, that Jehovah is very tender in affection and merciful.

---

course of endurance in favor of one of complaint and grumbling against God or their brothers. They faithfully and lovingly tried to help them. Jeremiah, for example, spoke kindly and with concern for King Zedekiah, even after Zedekiah had turned him over to the princes of Judah to be thrown into a cistern. Because Zedekiah's life was in great danger at the time, Jeremiah urged: "Obey, please, the voice of Jehovah in what I am speaking to you, and it will go well with you, and your soul will continue to live." (Jer. 38:20)

11 Look! We pronounce happy those who have endured

We call everyone who has persevered in the face of trials, and especially when he has done it with patience, a happy person, one who has Jehovah's blessing. Jesus said: "Happy are you when people reproach you and persecute you and lyingly say every sort of wicked thing against you for my sake. Rejoice and leap for joy, since your reward is great in the heavens; for in that way they persecuted the prophets prior to you." (Matt. 5:11, 12) This fact should comfort those who are in trials, hardships or tribulations, and should strengthen them to keep on serving God with patience. If we count such persons happy, we can achieve happiness in the same way.

You have heard of the endurance of Job

Job is an outstanding example of courageous endurance. All of James' readers had heard of Job or had read the Bible account. Job was not

an Israelite, yet he was accepted by the Jews as a faith-building example. The book of Job was recorded, no doubt, to show the reason why God allows his servants to suffer, and also to reveal his care for them. (Job 1:7-22; 2:6-10)

and have seen the outcome Jehovah gave

After Job had proved his trustworthiness and loyalty under extreme conditions of suffering, God rewarded him in several ways: Job gained a better understanding of God and his purpose. Job was caused to see God's majesty, power and justice, his almightiness and wisdom. (Job 40:6-14; 42:2) Also, God expressed his approval of Job before Job's three reproved companions. He directed these companions that, in order to get into good standing with Him, they would have to have the prayers of Job in their behalf. (Job 42:7, 8) Jehovah restored Job to health and extended his life for 140 years, giving Job 10 children and a double amount of material possessions. (Job 42:10-17) Moreover, Job's respect and dignity were

12 Above all things, though, my brothers, stop swearing, yes, either by heaven or by earth or by any other oath. But let your *Yes* mean Yes, and your *No*, No, so that you do not fall under judgment.

---

also restored. God mentioned Job as an outstandingly righteous man in Ezekiel 14:14, 20. He is certainly among the faithful men of old and looked forward to a resurrection. (Job 14:13-15)

that Jehovah is very tender in affection and merciful

Though Job lacked full understanding of the reason for his trials, and therefore indulged in some wrong reasoning, he remained loyal to God, steadfastly refusing to deny God or blame him with injustice. (Job 1:21, 22; 2:9, 10) God's upholding Job in endurance, forgiving Job his shortcomings, and the rich reward to Job at the end of the trial, showed deep appreciation for Job's faithfulness and great compassion and mercy on the part of Jehovah. (Ex. 34:6; Ps. 103:8) Job repented over the erroneous things he said during his dialogue. (Job 42:1-7)

Accordingly, Christians should take comfort in the fact that God will do the same for them if they persevere with patience and keep their hearts clean and firmly fixed on Jehovah. We can be sure that he will care for us and bring us to our goal, just as he did with Job and with other faithful men. (Mic. 7:18, 19)

12 Above all things, though, my brothers, stop swearing

James doubtless had in mind the words of Jesus: "Do not swear at all, neither by heaven, because it is God's throne; nor by earth, because it is the footstool of his feet; nor by Jerusalem, because it is the city of the great King. Nor by your head must you swear, because you cannot turn one hair white or black. Just let your word *Yes* mean Yes, your *No,* No; for

Admonition Against Swearing

what is in excess of these is from the wicked one." (Matt. 5:34-37)

By the expression "above all things," James does not mean to say that forbearance from swearing is the most important of all things. Rather, he meant that, whatever else they did, they should by no means indulge in such swearing, inasmuch as by swearing in that manner they would be stumbling in the use of the tongue and so would be sinning, the idle and unprofitable words being "from the wicked one." Hence, James does not refer to oaths such as may be required in a court of law, or on certain occasions of a very weighty and serious nature.

yes, either by heaven or by earth or by any other oath

These specific things, heaven and earth, were mentioned by James, as Jesus did, because the Pharisees allowed swearing by almost anything except by God.*

Jesus pointed out that swearing by the things that God has created or by what he owns is not only valueless, but also displeasing to God. Such swearing was a mere artifice or expedient in order for one not to be actually guilty of

---

* In *The International Critical Commentary,* on The Letter of James, page 302, commentator Ropes says: "Philo [a Jewish writer] discusses oaths . . . His principle is that oaths are to be avoided when possible, that oaths should be taken by lower objects ('the earth, the sun, the stars, the universe') rather than by 'the highest and eldest Cause,' and he praises the man who by any evasion (*cf.* [compare] English, 'Oh My!') avoids the utterance of the sacred words of oaths. His abhorrence of oaths is due to their profane impiety and unseemliness, but he also lays stress on truthfulness and on the wickedness of false swearing and of swearing to do wrong." So from this Jewish writer we see that minor restrictions were made on oaths, but they were, nevertheless, widely used among the Jews, contrary to Jesus' words.

13 Is there anyone suffering evil among you? Let him carry on prayer. Is there anyone in good spirits? Let him sing psalms.

---

using God's name frivolously or to no good purpose. Such swearing was used to make the swearer's words seem more serious or truthful, but actually it could make the hearers suspicious of the honesty and sincerity of the swearer. The man who is always swearing by this and swearing by that makes it evident that he is a rash, unstable and unreliable person. (Matt. 23:16-22)

But let your *Yes* mean Yes, and your *No*, No

The straightforward, direct, plain and definite answer is much more convincing and impressive, conveys more honesty, and does not involve the person in exaggerations, vain talk and situations that may later cause the speaker much trouble and embarrassment. (2 Cor. 1:17) Furthermore, when a Christian engages in thoughtless, frivolous oaths, people will be far less inclined to believe what he says when he is bearing witness to God and his purposes through Christ. For one to use God's name indiscriminately or lightly, or to be continually affirming statements with oaths, smacks of hypocrisy and turns others away from the form of worship that one advocates. Also, when such a Christian is required to take an oath in a serious matter, as in a court of law, the credibility of his testimony is weakened.

so that you do not fall under judgment

Jesus said that indiscriminate oaths are from the wicked one, and therefore James tells us that they can bring us under judgment from God.

13 Is there anyone suffering evil among you?

James here may well have had in mind what

he said earlier about following the pattern of the
prophets, who suffered much. The apostle Paul
encouraged Timothy to "suffer

Prayer Needed
in Good
Times and Bad

evil, do the work of an evan-
gelizer, fully accomplish your
ministry." (2 Tim. 4:5) Christians should not be discouraged
over affliction of any kind,
knowing that God can work out all things to their
benefit. (Rom. 8:28) They should turn to God,
the source of all comfort. (2 Cor. 1:3-5)

Let him carry on prayer

The examples of the faithful men of old and
of Jesus himself point us to prayer, especially
when we are making serious decisions or undergoing any trial. (Luke 6:12, 13) Jesus prayed
"with strong outcries and tears" in the garden of
Gethsemane on the night before his death. (Heb.
5:7; Luke 22:39-46) The apostle Peter assured
us that "the eyes of Jehovah are upon the righteous ones, and his ears are toward their supplication." (1 Pet. 3:12) And the apostle Paul en-
couragingly says: "Rejoice in the hope. Endure
under tribulation. Persevere in prayer." (Rom.
12:12; compare Psalm 107:6, 13, 28.) The way
of prayer is always open, with our great High
Priest always ready to plead for us, and the as-
surance of God's own affection toward us. (Heb.
7:25; 4:15, 16; John 16:26, 27)

Is there anyone in good spirits?

If the Christian is cheerful, in a good mental
state (literally, "is being well in spirit," *Kingdom
Interlinear Translation*),

Let him sing psalms

Our cheerfulness should not be turned into reck-
less merriment, but we should be balanced, moderate, and feel happy that God has blessed us,

14 Is there anyone sick among you? Let him call the older men of the congregation to him, and let them pray over him, greasing him with oil in the name of Jehovah.

---

at least for the time being, with freedom from tribulations. We could sing psalms. The psalms were set to music and were sung in the temple by the Levites and others. (2 Chron. 5:12; Ezra 2:64, 65) Certain songs (psalms) were sung during the celebration of the Passover, and Christ and his apostles sang these on the evening of Jesus' observance of the Passover and his institution of the Memorial. (Mark 14:26) The Greek word *psallō,* meaning to play a stringed instrument, then came to apply to singing to the accompaniment of such an instrument (for example, the harp). The word is used at Romans 15:9: "To your name I will make *melody.*" (Ps. 18:49; see Greek *Septuagint Version.*) Such singing does not have to be vocal, nor accompanied with literal music. At 1 Corinthians 14:15 the apostle Paul says that he will *sing praise* with the spirit and also with the mind. And at Ephesians 5:19 he exhorts Christians to speak "to yourselves with psalms and praises to God and spiritual songs, singing and accompanying yourselves with *music in your hearts* to Jehovah."

14 Is there anyone sick among you?

James has spoken about the general suffering of evil that Christians undergo, but here he turns to a specific problem often encountered by those who have once started in the right way, namely, spiritual weakness or sickness, of whatever type and from whatever cause. While many of Christendom's Bible commentators apply James' words to physical sickness, one noted scholar states the following: "The literal construction involves these surprising moments: 1. The calling for the presbyters of the congregation in the Plural; 2. the general direction concerning their prayer accompanying unction with oil; 3. and especially the confident promise that the prayer of faith shall restore the sick apart from his restoration being connected with the forgiveness of his sins. Was [James] warranted to promise bodily recovery in every case in which a sick individual complied with his directions? This misgiving urges us to adopt the symbolical construction of the passage, which would be as follows: if any man as a Christian has been hurt or become sick in his Christianity, let him seek healing from the presbyters, the kernel of the congregation. Let these pray with and for him and anoint him with the oil of the Spirit; such a course wherever taken, will surely restore him and his transgressions will be forgiven him."*

The spiritual sickness may be due to some wrong attitude or conduct, or to a failure to feed regularly at Jehovah's table. It appears that there were such erring ones in the Christian congregation at Corinth, concerning whom the apostle Paul wrote: "For he that eats and drinks eats and drinks judgment against himself if he does not discern the body. That is why many among you are weak and sickly, and quite a few are sleeping in death." (1 Cor. 11:29, 30) Other symptoms of the spiritual malady may be: Deep depression, isolation of oneself, doubt about Jehovah's direction of his people, a feeling of alienation from God, a sense of not being worthy enough to approach Jehovah in prayer. At times such spiritual weakness may even induce physical sickness. Is there any reason for a congregation member who has weakened spiritually to feel

* *Commentary on the Holy Scriptures,* by J. P. Lange (Zondervan), Vol. 12, p. 138.

hesitant about seeking the aid of elders so as to be strengthened and fortified against any future slipping back into wrongdoing or wrong thinking? The disciple James counsels:

Let him call the older men of the congregation to him

The older men are mature spiritual men, those assigned to serve as shepherds, of whom it is written: "Moreover, they appointed older men [to office] for them in each congregation and, offering prayer with fastings, they committed them to Jehovah in whom they had become believers." (Acts 14:23) And to the older men of the congregation at Ephesus the apostle Paul gave this exhortation: "Pay attention to yourselves and to all the flock, among which the holy spirit has appointed you overseers, to shepherd the congregation of God, which he purchased with the blood of his own Son." (Acts 20:28) It would not mean that all the elders must be called, since some of them might not be available at the specific time of need. And since the older men would not always be aware of the spiritual sickness, it would be the sick person's privilege to initiate things by asking for the elders to visit and assist him. If he were in a location far from his congregation, he might call elders from a nearby congregation. He would not call the elders with a view to having some argument with them, or for the purpose of defending his own position, for he would be aware of the fact that he was not in a spiritually healthy state. Rather, he would want to state his condition and seek their help and guidance in order to regain spiritual health.

and let them pray over him, greasing him with oil in the name of Jehovah

Prayer is seen to be the important part of the

action by the elders, since Jehovah hears "the prayer of the righteous ones." (Prov. 15:29) And like soothing oil the comforting reminders from the Holy Scriptures expressed by the elders would have the effect of allaying the fears and quieting the doubts of the ailing one. (Ps. 23:5; Jer. 8:22) Good, comforting conversation, "healthful words," and the reading of the Bible to the sick one will greatly encourage him, like the rubbing in of soothing, literal oil. (Isa. 61:3; compare 2 Timothy 1:13; Titus 2:1.) Often, upon hearing the fervent, heartfelt prayer offered by the elders in his behalf, the distressed one himself will be strengthened to draw close to Jehovah in prayer. He may be helped to reason that if others are confident that Jehovah will answer prayers in his behalf, then he too can share that confidence. The elders would remind him of Jehovah's great mercy and His willingness to hear the prayer of the lowly and contrite one, even as the Scriptures testify: "Jehovah is near to those that are broken at heart; and those who are crushed in spirit he saves." —Ps. 34:18; see also Nehemiah 9:17b.

In harmony with their prayers for his recovery, the elders would also take steps to see that assistance to the sick one would be extended over a period of time. Today that would include making arrangements to have someone study regularly with the spiritual invalid until he had recovered his spiritual health. They would also encourage the sickly one to become once more a joyful member of the Kingdom-preaching congregation.

All such action on the part of the older men is done "in the name of Jehovah," and this would mean that they would not lean on their own ideas as to the needs of the sick one. Rather, they would apply Jehovah's counsel or correction, expressing

15 And the prayer of faith will make the indisposed one well, and Jehovah will raise him up. Also, if he has committed sins, it will be forgiven him.

Jehovah's mind on the matter that has produced the problem.

15 And the prayer of faith will make the indisposed one well, and Jehovah will raise him up

Were we to apply this passage and context to the treatment of physical sickness or weakness, it could not be definitely stated that the person would be strengthened or cured. But when applied to a spiritual indisposition, it is clear that Jehovah would aid the humble, repentant one, the one showing willingness to be aided by his Word and spirit, to make a spiritual comeback, thus raising him up to renewed spiritual health.

In order for "the prayer of faith" offered by the elders to be efficacious, it would need to be backed up by faith on the part of the sickly one. Christians pray with the understanding that "no matter what it is that we ask according to his will, he hears us." (1 John 5:14) And Jesus said: "All the things you ask in prayer, having faith, you will receive." (Matt. 21:22) He also promised: "If you ask anything in my name, I will do it." (John 14:14) So "the prayer of faith" is the prayer that is 'according to God's will' or 'in Jesus' name,' that is, something that would be approved or authorized by Christ Jesus.

Also, if he has committed sins, it will be forgiven him

Spiritual distress or sickness often results from some wrong attitude or practice that places one at variance with Jehovah. The conscience of the

16 Therefore openly confess your sins to one another and pray for one another, that you may get healed. A righteous man's supplication, when it is at work, has much force.

---

sick one may be chastising him, or he may feel so deeply enmeshed in wrongdoing that he doubts that there will be any forgiveness. He may feel unworthy to approach Jehovah and may be so distracted that he cannot concentrate sufficiently to formulate even some simple prayer. Where there is such distress the elders will lovingly apply the soothing, corrective counsel of the Scriptures. Once they had discerned the nature of the trouble, they would point out to the sick one the proper course he must take in order to achieve a cure. Particularly if the person revealed that he had committed sins, would the older men make clear the wrongness of some course or attitude, and this would result in a chastening or reproving of the ailing one. On this point David wrote: "Should the righteous one strike me, it would be a loving-kindness; and should he reprove me, it would be oil upon the head, which my head would not want to refuse." (Ps. 141:5) "Show me favor, O Jehovah, for I am fading away. Heal me, O Jehovah, for my bones have been disturbed. Yes, my own soul has been very much disturbed; and you, O Jehovah—how long? Do return, O Jehovah, do rescue my soul; save me for the sake of your loving-kindness." (Ps. 6:2-4) Jehovah will look kindly upon such a humble, honest one, and upon the prayers of the elders in his behalf, and will forgive his sins and restore him to spiritual health.

16 Therefore openly confess your sins to one another and pray for one another

How encouraging toward 'openly confessing sins to one another' if the sincerely repentant wrong-doer knows that those to whom he confesses are primarily interested in helping him 'get healed'

Loving Aid to Overcome Sin

of his spiritual sickness! However, if such a repentant one felt that the elders would automatically deal with him as one meriting a reprimand before the whole congregation as a 'practicer of sin,' the effect would be quite different. Such a feeling could create a barrier between the congregational shepherds and those sorely needing their help to overcome a drift into continued wrongdoing. On the other hand, where confidence existed that the elders would take into account one's sincerity in wanting to turn away from the wrong course or attitude, being desirous of never going back to it, this would surely be an encouragement to call upon the older men for assistance, and to respond to their help as would an ailing sheep to that of its conscientious shepherd.—Contrast Psalm 23:1-5 with Ezekiel 34:4.

The tense of the Greek verbs used here has a continuative sense, as saying, 'Make it a practice to confess openly your sins to one another.' Thus, Phillips' *The New Testament in Modern English* reads: "You should get into the habit of admitting your sins to each other."

James has previously dealt with matters that exemplify the family-like interest and warm concern that should exist within the Christian congregation as a brotherhood. With such a spiritual atmosphere, there should indeed be a confidence among its members that contributes to freeness of expression, and that confidence could be especially notable when it came to acknowledging one's faults and wrong acts. Christians are shown in Scripture that they can and should have freeness of speech in going to God with their petitions and problems, for they have a loving

Father and a compassionate, understanding Helper with the Father, God's Son. (Heb. 2:17, 18; 4:14-16; 1 John 2:1, 2; 3:19-21; 4:17-19) What is true of the heavenly courts should be reflected in the earthly realm of God's servants.

This confessing is not like a "confessional" arrangement where one is viewed as obligated to appear and confess all sins in order to obtain absolution from guilt in the eyes of God. Although James had previously made specific mention of the congregation elders with regard to sick ones needing aid, he here says to "confess your sins to one another," not limiting the matter to certain ones within the congregation. While this is so, it is reasonable that the one confessing his sins would seek a person who could be of real help to him in a spiritual way. Along with the desire to unburden himself, he doubtless desires the counsel and prayer of another. Galatians 6:1, 2 speaks of the readjusting of one who takes a false step and shows that it is those "who have spiritual qualifications" who are in a position to do this. Elders should have such qualifications, and others in the congregation may also have these. A woman, for example, may seek the help of a Christian sister, possibly someone older than she is, as is indicated by Paul's counsel at Titus 2:3-5. Thus the source of the help is not limited to a certain few; the important thing is that the person have "spiritual qualifications." James shows that the object and result of this humble seeking for help should be a brotherly (or a sisterly) interest manifested in prayer to Jehovah on behalf of the one confessing the fault.

The expression "to one another" is most appropriate since all must honestly recognize their own sinful nature, thereby eliminating any basis for pride or superiority in responding to the needs of the erring one. (Compare Luke 18:9-14;

1 John 1:8-10.) Rather than superiority, there obviously should be a sense of mutual compassion, all having their own particular faults and weaknesses. The one extending help now should realize that he may someday need help himself. Along with calling for humility, such open confessing of faults can also serve as a restraint toward sinning. It leads away from a secretive course of life that deprives one of the balancing effect that the counsel of others can provide.

that you may get healed

One who has been spiritually sick or downhearted because of some sin may call for the healing help of another brother's prayer. It may be that he has let the sin become a barrier to his freeness of speech in approaching God in prayer. (Compare Lamentations 3:44.) He may, along with his bad spiritual state, be also physically sick. In fact, the sickness may be partly due to his spiritual lack. The prayer of the brother for him may help him not only in a spiritual sense, but also in a physical way.

A righteous man's supplication, when it is at work, has much force

James has been stressing prayer, especially intercessory prayers for others. He encourages the congregation to give yet greater attention to prayers for one another. The apostle Paul advocates supplicatory prayers for others. He says: "I therefore exhort, first of all, that supplications, prayers, intercessions, offerings of thanks, be made concerning all sorts of men." (1 Tim. 2:1) Paul urged the congregations to pray for himself and his co-workers. (2 Thess. 3:1; Col. 4:2-4) James speaks of a "righteous" man, which would be anyone in the congregation who had exercised true faith in God and the Lord Jesus Christ, and who, therefore, was counted righteous with God.

17 Elijah was a man with feelings like ours, and yet in prayer he prayed for it not to rain; and it did not rain upon the land for three years and six months.

There is power in prayer. It accomplishes much with God. The person who is righteous in the sight of God is accepted by Him, and his prayers are heard. The apostle Peter said: "The eyes of Jehovah are upon the righteous ones, and his ears are toward their supplication." (1 Pet. 3:12) The apostle John described the efficacy of prayer, saying: "This is the confidence that we have toward him, that, no matter what it is that we ask according to his will, he hears us. Further, if we know he hears us respecting whatever we are asking, we know we are to have the things asked since we have asked them of him." (1 John 5:14, 15) And the fact that prayer for a brother can mean life to him is shown by John: "If anyone catches sight of his brother sinning a sin that does not incur death, he will ask, and he will give life to him." (1 John 5:16) Thus, everyone in the congregation (as John says, "anyone") should show this loving concern for such an erring one, approaching God in prayer on his behalf.

James now proceeds to give a powerful example of the force of a righteous man's prayer, and points out that any member of the congregation in good standing with God can have confidence in the effectualness of his prayers. Also, the one needing the intercessory prayer can have like confidence. He writes:

17 Elijah was a man with feelings like ours

James points to the example of Elijah, evidently because Elijah was very highly esteemed by the Jews. Some of them thought that Jesus was Elijah returned. (Matt. 16:14) Elijah was considered to be representative of the line of prophets. (He appeared in this capacity in the transfiguration vision. [Mark 9:4]) When Jesus, dying on the stake, called out *"Eli, Eli, lama sabachthani?"* ("My God, my God, why have you forsaken me?"), the Jews thought that he was calling Elijah. (Mark 15:34, 35) James says that Elijah was a man with feelings like ours, meaning that,

though he was a prophet, and was given power to work miracles, he had the same human feelings, weaknesses and sensations that all men have. For he was not always giving inspired prophecy or working miracles, and, when doing so, was doing these things, not in his own power or by his personal goodness, but by God's spirit working in connection with him. (Compare 1 Kings 17:20-22.) It would follow, therefore, that if this one, whom the Jews regarded so highly, had feelings like all men, then all the prophets felt likewise. They were not supernatural men. (Compare Acts 14:15, where the apostle Paul and Barnabas speak similarly of themselves.)

Peter and John were also men with feelings like ours. Accordingly Peter said to the people who saw the healing of a lame man take place: "Men of Israel, why are you wondering over this, or why are you gazing at us as though by *personal power* or *godly devotion* we have made him walk?" (Acts 3:12) There was no power inherent in Peter or John of themselves, and their healing ability was not because of their being such surpassingly "good" or devoted men. It was because of their *faith in the name of Jesus Christ* that Christ supplied power to heal the man. Consequently, any righteous man in the congregation could help another by his prayers.

and yet in prayer he prayed for it not to rain

The Hebrew Scriptures themselves do not make specific mention of Elijah's praying for it not to rain, although he did announce the drought in advance. (1 Ki. 17:1) But Elijah was a man of prayer, who petitioned God with regard to the fire test in the contest with the Baal prophets, and was answered by a miracle of God. (1 Ki. 18:36-38) Jehovah made the promise of rain, in 1 Kings 18:1; this was an encouragement to Elijah to pray for it to end the drought. And that Elijah did pray is implied at 1 Kings 18:42: "As for Elijah, he went up to the top of Carmel and began crouching to the earth and keeping his face put between his knees." Certainly all the prophets accomplished their acts in God's name and through their faith and relationship and communication with God. The example of Elijah's prayers in withholding and sending rain is a powerful one, and James was inspired and not mistaken in attributing the miracle to the power of prayer.

and it did not rain upon the land for three years and six months

James here speaks of three and a half years of no rain. The account in 1 Kings 18:1 refers to rain coming in the "third year," possibly meaning in the third year of actual drought. The dry summer season in Israel lasts for six months, from April to September. So, it would seem that, following upon this, three continuous years of drought ensued, making a total of three and a half years with no rain. The *rain itself* had stopped three and a half years previously, so that it was actually three and a half years from rain to rain. However, while the drought could be counted as from the time the rain ceased, it may not have been genuinely noticeable and distressful until the streams began drying up and a real want of water was experienced, perhaps some six months later. Even though the rain had stopped, the people could live on the preceding year's harvest for quite a long period before they really felt the drought; and this may be the reason for the expression "in the third year," at 1 Kings 18:1, rather than 'the fourth year.' But we have the best authority of all in Jesus Christ, who said "the heaven was shut up three years and six months, so that a great famine fell upon all the land." (Luke 4:25)

18 And he prayed again, and the heaven gave rain and the land put forth its fruit.

19 My brothers, if anyone among you is misled from the truth and another turns him back,

---

18 And he prayed again, and the heaven gave rain and the land put forth its fruit

By this notable example James succeeds in illustrating the great power of prayer by any righteous man, if offered according to the will of God.

19 My brothers, if anyone among you is misled from the truth

"The truth" would include both doctrine or teachings, and moral conduct. It is what we believe in our hearts about God and Christ that makes us what we are as Christians. The true teaching about God and Christ precedes the moral conduct, and is that upon which all right action is based. Jesus said: "This means everlasting life, their taking in knowledge of [or, "knowing"] you, the only true God, and of the one whom you sent forth, Jesus Christ." (John 17:3) James views God's word as truth, and so the written Word now contains all truth necessary for Christians. He says that anointed Christians are brought forth by "the word of truth . . . to be certain firstfruits of his creatures." (Jas. 1:18)

A Christian may wander away from the path of truth. Whereas he has "passed over from death to life," he may be drifting back toward darkness and death. (1 John 3:14) It is the duty of any Christian, not just the elders, to help him to recover. We are told: "Brothers, even though a man takes some false step before he is aware of it, you who have spiritual qualifications try to readjust such a man in a spirit of mildness, as you each keep an eye on yourself, for fear you

20 know that he who turns a sinner back from
the error of his way will save his soul from death
and will cover a multitude of sins.

---

also may be tempted." (Gal. 6:1) In giving counsel to help one who is misled, James is following
his closing theme on the importance and power
of prayer. It takes diligent application of God's
Word and earnest prayer to accomplish the recovery of an erring one. If help is not given, the
individual can go so far as to be beyond repentance. He would then not desire to repent and
return to the true worship of God, and that desire
could not be rekindled. (Heb. 6:4-8; 10:26-29)

and another turns him back

A Christian who has been misled from the
truth, either by wrong doctrinal thinking of his
own, or as led by someone else, or by moral
aberration, is in a dangerous position. The expression "turns him back" denotes that a sinner
who is still of the world, never having accepted
the truth, is *not* the person being discussed; it is
a Christian who has deviated from the truth
that he once believed and followed.

Jesus showed the care for his disciples that we
should have for one another. He said to Peter,
when telling Peter that Satan desired to have the
apostles in order to sift them as wheat, and before saying that Peter would deny him: "I have
made supplication for you that your faith may
not give out; and you, when once you have *returned,* strengthen your brothers." (Luke 22:32)
In this passage the same Greek word is used
with regard to the recovery of the erring person.
This is indeed a loving act.

20 know that he who turns a sinner back from

the error of his way will save his soul from death

The word "know" emphasizes the importance and weightiness of this work of reclaiming the sinning one. It is something of which we should really be thoroughly aware. The soul that is saved from death is the sinner himself, not the one doing the helping. It is true that we benefit from the good work that we do, but no works can save our souls from death. Only the atonement sacrifice of Jesus Christ can do that. There is no substitute. (Acts 4:12) The person saved was going in the way toward death; he was in great danger of death, spiritual death, which would mean eternal death for him. By causing him to turn back, the Christian who extends love and counsel, prayer and other help, thereby keeps the erring one under the atonement sacrifice of Christ, and that one is thereby saved from condemnation and death.

and will cover a multitude of sins

The sins covered are those of the erring one. Jehovah entreated the nation of Israel to return to him, so that "though the sins of you people should prove to be as scarlet, they will be made white just like snow; though they should be red like crimson cloth, they will become even like wool." (Isa. 1:18) The one doing the recovery work does not get his own sins forgiven by this act. He can get forgiveness for his sins only through confession to God and prayer for forgiveness on the basis of Christ's sacrifice. The apostle Peter wrote: "Love covers a multitude of sins [of the one toward whom loving help is expressed]." (1 Pet. 4:8)

If we felt that, by helping a brother in this way, we received a covering for our own sins, we might tend to think that we could work out our own righteousness, which would be a serious mistake. (Compare Romans 10:2, 3.) It would cause us to see less clearly the great atonement work of Jesus Christ and, instead of exercising faith in him, we would feel that it was our merit that works out our salvation.

One who loves his brother will cover that one's sins by not advertising them to others. (Prov. 10:12) But James does not refer to this kind of covering. He means that when the one who has been misled from the truth is reproved by his brother, seeing the wrongness of the way he is going, turns back and repents, asking God to forgive him, the reprover has worked toward the covering over of that one's sins. The recovered one will experience what David described: "Happy is the one whose revolt is pardoned, *whose sin is covered.* Happy is the man to whose account Jehovah does not put error." (Ps. 32:1, 2) Of course, God does see the loving work being done, and certainly will reward the one doing it. (2 Cor. 5:10; compare Colossians 3:23, 24; Luke 14:13, 14.)

With this final exposition on the value of prayer, and on the deep love and concern each member of the congregation must have for each of the others, James closes this fine letter.

QUESTIONS FOR STUDY

VERSE 1

Come, now, you rich men

1 Is James here speaking to all rich men?
2 Why would James address such men in a letter to congregations?
3 What parallel do we have for James' doing this?
4 What was the danger to Christians as they viewed the material prosperity of the rich?
5 How does the counsel of James have the same purpose as the counsel of the 73rd Psalm, written by Asaph?

weep, howling over your miseries that are coming upon you

1 What sort of weeping and howling is here referred to?

2 When is the weeping to take place?

3 How did their wealth deceive the possessors of riches?

4 What is the twofold purpose of James' counsel regarding riches?

VERSE 2

Your riches have rotted

1 What constituted a substantial part of wealth in James' day?

2 What did James mean by saying that their riches had rotted?

3 In *speaking* of riches rotting, is James emphasizing particularly the perishableness of wealth, or what?

and your outer garments have become moth-eaten

1 Why does James mention garments in this context?

VERSE 3

Your gold and silver are rusted away

1 Why is the expression "rusted away" used here?

and their rust will be as a witness against you

1 Why and how is the rust "a witness" against them?

and will eat your fleshy parts

1 What is the fearsome picture that James draws here?

Something like fire is what you have stored up in the last days

1 What is the situation of all mankind since the coming of Christ to earth, as regards the "good news"?

2 What is the fire here spoken of, and when will this fire come upon these wicked rich men?

VERSE 4

Look! The wages due the workers who harvested your fields but which are held up by you, keep crying out

1 How did these rich men demonstrate their greediness?

2 How did the withheld wages "keep crying out"?

and the calls for help on the part of the reapers have entered into the ears of Jehovah of armies

1 Whether the defrauded workers cried out directly to God or not, how can it be said their cries entered into the ears of Jehovah?

2 How did the Mosaic law legislate specifically against such fraudulent treatment of workers?

3 In this connection, what is significant about the use of the title "Jehovah of armies"?

VERSE 5

You have lived in luxury upon the earth

    1 What is the sense in which they have lived "in luxury"?

and have gone in for sensual pleasure

    1 What is the force of the expression "sensual pleasure"?

    2 To what can going in for sensual pleasure lead a person?

You have fattened your hearts on the day of slaughter

    1 How and with what attitude were these wicked rich men 'fattening their hearts on the day of slaughter'?

VERSE 6

You have condemned, you have murdered the righteous one

    1 Whom does James mean by "the righteous one"?

    2 What outstanding crime may James also have had in mind when writing?

    3 How does the psalmist express the same thought?

Is he not opposing you?

    1 To what does this question refer?

    2 What does the Greek term for "opposing," as used in the Scriptures, imply?

    3 How did the conduct of Jesus and his disciples give no basis for persecuting them?

    4 Why is the righteous course of God's servants never in vain?

VERSE 7

Exercise patience, therefore, brothers, until the presence of the Lord

    1 Up to this point, what sins of the rich had James described?

    2 Why would James tell Christians to exercise patience?

    3 Why was it worth while for Christians to await with patience the presence of the Lord?

    4 Why was it necessary to tell Christians of the first century to exercise patience until the presence of the Lord, when his presence would not occur in their lifetime?

Look! The farmer keeps waiting for the precious fruit of the earth

1 How does the farmer exercise patience waiting for his crop?

exercising patience over it until he gets the early rain and the late rain
1 In Palestine, when were the early and the late rains?

VERSE 8

You too exercise patience; make your hearts firm, because the presence of the Lord has drawn close
1 In what ways, particularly, should Christians exercise patience?
2 Why is the keeping of a firm heart so important?

VERSE 9

Do not heave sighs against one another, brothers
1 Is James here speaking especially of talking against or slandering others?
2 Their knowing what things will keep a Christian from groaning and sighing deeply against one another?

so that you do not get judged
1 How and why would the Christian be judged for 'heaving sighs' at his brothers?

Look! The Judge is standing before the doors
1 In what way can it be said that "the Judge is standing before the doors"?
2 If a Christian should let his impatience cause him to begin to groan and heave sighs against his brothers, what would be the result to him?

VERSE 10

Brothers, take as a pattern of the suffering of evil and the exercising of patience the prophets, who spoke in the name of Jehovah
1 Why does James here call attention to the prophets?
2 How did Jeremiah exemplify the exercising of patience under evil?

VERSE 11

Look! We pronounce happy those who have endured
1 How is it that we "pronounce happy those who have endured"?
2 What effect should this fact have upon us?

You have heard of the endurance of Job
1 Why did James call attention to Job?

and have seen the outcome Jehovah gave
1 What better understanding of God did **Job gain** because of his endurance under suffering?

2 What other rewards did Job receive as a result of his endurance?

that Jehovah is very tender in affection and merciful
  1 How did Jehovah show great mercy in the case of Job?
  2 What encouragement can the account about Job give us?

VERSE 12

Above all things, though, my brothers, stop swearing
  1 What words of Jesus did James undoubtedly have in mind?
  2 What does James mean by the expression "above all things"?

yes, either by heaven or by earth or by any other oath
  1, and footnote. How did the Jews, at the time Jesus was on earth, regard the making of oaths?
  2 Why is swearing by the things God has created a bad thing to do?
  3 What effect does the indiscriminate making of oaths have upon a person's reputation?

But let your "Yes" mean Yes, and your "No," No
  1 Why is straightforward and direct speech far superior to the making of oaths?
  2 What effect does the Christian who makes rash or frivolous oaths have on others' view of his form of worship?
  3 What similar effect would this have in a court of law?

so that you do not fall under judgment
  1 Why does a person making indiscriminate oaths fall under judgment?

VERSE 13

Is there anyone suffering evil among you?
  1 Should a Christian think it strange if he suffers evil? How should he view it?

Let him carry on prayer
  1 What encouragement and what examples do we have of the value of carrying on prayer when undergoing evil conditions?

Is there anyone in good spirits?
  1 What does this expression mean?

Let him sing psalms
  1 When a Christian is in good spirits, in what way should this cheerfulness be displayed?
  2 Does the singing of praises to God have to be audible?

VERSE 14

Is there anyone sick among you?

    1 Besides other forms of suffering evil, what specific problem may be encountered by Christians?

    2 What may be the causes and symptoms of the spiritual weakness?

Let him call the older men of the congregation to him

    1 Who are the older men here mentioned?

    2 Who should take the initiative in getting the elders to visit the sick one?

    3 With what attitude would the sick one receive the elders?

and let them pray over him, greasing him with oil in the name of Jehovah

    1 What is the most important part of the help that elders give?

    2 Their use of the symbolic "oil" would have what effect on the sick one?

    3 What other help might elders extend?

    4 In what way is their action "in the name of Jehovah"?

VERSE 15

And the prayer of faith will make the indisposed one well, and Jehovah will raise him up

    1 When applied to physical sickness, what difficulty arises here?

    2 What is "the prayer of faith" that truly benefits the sick one?

Also, if he has committed sins, it will be forgiven him

    1 What may be responsible for spiritual distress or sickness?

    2 What wrong thinking may assail the sick one?

    3 How can the reproving counsel of the elders be like oil to the one being reproved?

    4 Particularly if the individual revealed that he had committed certain sins, what would the elders do?

    5 What, then, will be the result of the elders' counsel and prayers?

VERSE 16

Therefore openly confess your sins to one another and pray for one another

    1 What would encourage the spiritually sick one to call for the elders?

    2 What might tend to place a barrier between him and the elders?

3 What does the tense of the Greek word used here for "confess" indicate?

4 What condition or attitude within the congregation would contribute to such open confessing of wrongs?

5 To whom is the confessing to be done and with what object in view?

6 Why is the expression "to one another" so appropriate here?

7 How can this open confessing act as a restraint to wrongdoing?

that you may get healed

1 Into what condition may the person's sin have brought him?

2 How may the prayer of a brother for him help him?

A righteous man's supplication, when it is at work, has much force

1 What do both James and the apostle Paul encourage Christians to do for one another?

2 Who is the "righteous" man to whom James refers?

3 How do we know that the prayers of one who is in good standing with God are answered?

4 To what extent may prayer for another help him?

5 How does James proceed to show that the one praying and the one prayed for can have confidence that they will receive an answer?

VERSE 17

Elijah was a man with feelings like ours

1 Why does James point to Elijah in this instance?

2 What did James mean by saying that Elijah had "feelings like ours"?

3 Did all the prophets, as well as the apostles, have like feelings?

4 How did Peter express the matter?

5 Therefore, what may we conclude about the value of prayer on the part of any faithful man in the congregation?

and yet in prayer he prayed for it not to rain

1 What evidence is there that the drought upon Israel in King Ahab's day was brought in answer to Elijah's prayer?

and it did not rain upon the land for three years and six months

1 Though the Hebrew Scripture account of the drought does not say specifically that it lasted

three and a half years, what evidence do we have
that this was the case?

VERSE 18

*And he prayed again, and the heaven gave rain and
the land put forth its fruit*
  1 What does this example definitely prove?

VERSE 19

*My brothers, if anyone among you is misled from the
truth*
  1 What does the expression "the truth" include?
  2 Why is it of such vital importance to pray for one
  who errs, or for one who strays from the path of
  truth?
  3 What may happen if someone does not help the
  erring one?

and another turns him back
  1 Is the person spoken of here one who is a member
  of the Christian congregation, or one who has not
  previously accepted the truth of the "good news"?
  2 How did Jesus show this kind of care for the
  apostle Peter?

VERSE 20

*know that he who turns a sinner back from the error
of his way will save his soul from death*
  1 Why are the brothers instructed to *know* this fact?
  2 Is the soul here saved the one who turns the sinner
  back? Why?
  3 Show that it is the sinner who is saved from death.

and will cover a multitude of sins
  1 Whose sins are covered?
  2 What would be the danger of believing that by
  helping others who have sinned, we would be covering our own sins?
  3 Does the covering of sin here referred to mean not
  advertising that one's sins?
  4 How are the sins covered?

Aid to Bible Understanding

This 1,700-page book lists, in its more than 4,000 alphabetically arranged entries, every significant subject in the Bible, discussing:

- **BIBLE LANDS**—Cities and villages of Israel and the nations that influenced their history
  The geography and climate of these lands, native trees and plants, birds and animals
- **PEOPLES**—Their customs and forms of religion, and their wars
- **NOTABLE EVENTS**—God's dealings with mankind through all periods of Bible history: Creation, the fall of Adam, the Flood, the Patriarchs, the Exodus and the giving of the Law, the turbulent history of Israel, Christ's life and ministry and the founding of the Christian congregation

You may obtain a copy of this fine **Aid to Bible Understanding** by remitting $7 (U.S.), postpaid

NEW WORLD TRANSLATION OF THE HOLY SCRIPTURES

A modern-language translation of the Bible from its original tongues—not a mere version or revision

- **RELIABLE**—Consistency in uniformly rendering the Hebrew expressions provides greater accuracy
- **UNDERSTANDABLE**—Modern language, paragraphed for easier reading and quicker grasp of the sense of the passage being read
- **REGULAR EDITION:** Hardback, green vinyl cover; abridged concordance, and maps. Available in English, Dutch, French, German, Italian, Portuguese, Spanish. Size: 7¼" X 4⅞" X 1⅛". $2 (U.S.), postpaid
- **LARGE-PRINT EDITION:** Revised in 1971; big easy-to-read type; hardback, black vinyl cover, footnotes, abridged concordance, maps. English, Spanish. Size: 7½" X 9½" X 1½". $5 (U.S.), postpaid

To order, use nearest address on the next page.

CHIEF OFFICE AND OFFICIAL ADDRESS OF
Watch Tower Bible and Tract Society of Pennsylvania
Watchtower Bible and Tract Society of New York, Inc.
International Bible Students Association
124 Columbia Heights, Brooklyn, New York 11201, U.S.A.
ADDRESSES OF BRANCH OFFICES:

ALASKA 99507: 2552 East 48th Ave., Anchorage. **AUSTRALIA:** 11 Beresford Road, Strathfield, N.S.W. 2135. **AUSTRIA:** Gallgasse 44, A-1130 Vienna. **BAHAMAS:** Box N-1247, Nassau, N.P. **BARBADOS:** Fontabelle Rd., Bridgetown. **BELGIUM:** rue d'Argile 60, B-1950 Kraainem. **BELIZE:** Box 257, Belize City. **BOLIVIA:** Casilla No. 1440, La Paz. **BRAZIL:** Rua Guaíra, 216, Bosque da Saúde, 04142 São Paulo, SP; Caixa Postal 12.896, 01000 São Paulo, SP. **BURMA:** P.O. Box 62, Rangoon. **CANADA M6A 1Z5:** 150 Bridgeland Ave., Toronto, Ontario. **CHILE:** Clorinda Wilshaw 501, Ñuñoa; Casilla 261-V, Santiago 21. **COLOMBIA:** Apartado Aereo 91346, Bogotá 8, D.E. **COSTA RICA:** Apartado 10043, San José. **CYPRUS:** P.O. Box 288, Limassol. **DENMARK:** Kongevejen 207, DK-2830 Virum. **DOMINICAN REPUBLIC:** Avenida Francia 33 (Apartado 1742), Santo Domingo. **ECUADOR:** Casilla 4512, Guayaquil. **EL SALVADOR:** Apartado 401, San Salvador. **ENGLAND:** Watch Tower House, The Ridgeway, London NW7 1RN. **FIJI:** Box 23, Suva. **FINLAND:** Postbox 68, SF-01301 Vantaa 30. **FRANCE:** 81 rue du Point-du-Jour, 92100 Boulogne-Billancourt. **GERMANY, FEDERAL REPUBLIC OF:** Postfach 5920, D-6200 Wiesbaden 1. **GHANA:** Box 760, Accra. **GREECE:** 77, Leoforos Kifisias—Paradisos, Amarousion, Athens. **GUADELOUPE:** B.P. 239, 97156 Pointe-á-Pitre Cedex. **GUATEMALA:** 11 Avenida 5-67, Guatemala 1. **GUYANA:** 50 Brickdam, Georgetown 16. **HAITI:** Post Box 185, Port-au-Prince. **HAWAII** 96814: 1228 Pensacola St., Honolulu. **HONDURAS:** Apartado 147, Tegucigalpa. **HONG KONG:** 312 Prince Edward Rd., Second Floor, Kowloon. **ICELAND:** Vardturninn Box 251, 121 Reykjavik. **INDIA:** Post Bag 10, Lonavla, Pune Dis., Mah. 410 401. **IRAN:** P.O. Box 11-1797, Tehran. **IRELAND:** 86 Lindsay Rd., Glasnevin, Dublin 9. **ISRAEL:** P.O. Box 44520, Haifa 31 040. **ITALY:** Via della Bufalotta 1281, 00138 Rome. **IVORY COAST:** 10 B.P. 250, Abidjan 10. **JAMAICA:** 41 Trafalgar Rd., Kingston 10. **JAPAN:** 5-5-8 Mita Minato-Ku, Tokyo, 108. **KENYA:** Box 47788, Nairobi. **KOREA:** Box 7 Sodaemun P.O., Seoul, 120. **LEEWARD ISLANDS:** Box 119, St. Johns, Antigua. **LIBERIA:** P.O. Box 171, Monrovia. **LUXEMBOURG:** 15, rue de l'Egalite, Luxembourg-Bonnevoie, G.D. **MALAYSIA:** 20 Scotland Close, Penang. **MARTINIQUE:** Alize 4, B-7 Floreal, 97200 Fort de France. **MAURITIUS:** 42 Vandermeersch St., Rose Hill. **MEXICO:** Apartado Postal 42-048, Mexico 4, D.F. **NETHERLANDS:** Voorburgstraat 250, 1059 VD Amsterdam. **NETHERLANDS ANTILLES:** Oosterbeekstraat 11, Willemstad, Curaçao. **NEW CALEDONIA:** B.P. 787, Nouméa. **NEWFOUNDLAND, CANADA A1C 2M1:** 239 Pennywell Rd., St. John's. **NEW ZEALAND:** 6-A Western Springs Road, Auckland 3. **NICARAGUA:** Apartado 183, Managua, D.N. **NIGERIA:** P.O. Box 194, Yaba, Lagos State. **NORWAY:** Inkognitogaten 28 B., Oslo 2. **OKINAWA JAPAN,** 901-13: 546 Itarashiki-ku, Yonabaru-Cho. **PAKISTAN:** 8-E Habibullah Rd., Lahore 3. **PANAMA:** Apartado 1386, Panama 1. **PAPUA NEW GUINEA:** Box 113, Port Moresby. **PERU:** Gervasio Santillana 370; Casilla 5178, Miraflores, Lima 18. **PHILIPPINES, REPUBLIC OF:** P.O. Box 2044, Manila 2800; 186 Roosevelt Ave., San Francisco del Monte, Quezon City 3010. **PORTUGAL:** Apartado 91, P-2766, Estoril Codex. **PUERTO RICO** 00927: Calle Onix 23, Urb. Bucaré, Rio Piedras. **RHODESIA:** 35 Fife Avenue, Salisbury. **SENEGAL:** B.P. 3107, Dakar. **SIERRA LEONE:** Box 136, Freetown. **SOLOMON ISLANDS:** P.O. Box 166, Honiara. **SOUTH AFRICA:** Private Bag 2, Elandsfontein, 1406. **SPAIN:** Calle Pardo 65, Barcelona 16. **SRI LANKA, REP. OF:** 62 Layard's Road, Colombo 5. **SURINAM:** Wicherstraat 8-10; Box 49, Paramaribo. **SWEDEN:** Box 8, S-175 21 Järfälla 1. **SWITZERLAND:** Ulmenweg 45; P.O. Box 477, CH-3601 Thun. **TAHITI:** B.P. 518, Papeete. **TAIWAN:** 106 (REPUBLIC OF CHINA): 5 Lane 99, Yun-Ho St., Taipei. **THAILAND:** 69/1 Soi 2, Sukhumvit Rd., Bangkok 11. **TRINIDAD:** 2 La Seiva Road, Maraval, Port of Spain. **UNITED STATES OF AMERICA:** 117 Adams St., Brooklyn, N.Y. 11201. **URUGUAY:** Francisco Bauzá 3372, Montevideo. **VENEZUELA:** Apartado 116, La Victoria, Edo. Aragua. **ZAIRE, REP. OF:** B.P. 634, Limete, Kinshasa. **ZAMBIA, REP. OF:** Box 1598, Kitwe.